T0368339

Waiting For Your Miracle

DR. MARK AND PARIS MCCONNELL

authorHOUSE

AuthorHouse™
1663 Liberty Drive
Bloomington, IN 47403
www.authorhouse.com
Phone: 833-262-8899

Published by AuthorHouse 01/31/2025

ISBN: 979-8-8230-4324-3 (sc)
ISBN: 979-8-8230-4323-6 (e)

Library of Congress Control Number: 2025901968

Foreword

Serving for 22 years as Pastor of Calvary Baptist Church, San Antonio, Texas and my second term as President of the Baptist Ministers Union, San Antonio and Vicinity, I have ministered to church members and others as I travel the city and state who are facing life challenges and hardships.

My friend and brother, Rev. Dr. Mark McConnell's book identifies scriptures and biblical principles you will want to depend on during suffering and hardships. As I recall many life experiences we shared together growing up and challenges through adulthood, I know he is the perfect one to pen this book. You will not want to put this book down as he takes you through his recent health crisis and the steps he took trusting God through his suffering.

As we navigate life and faith, there is always room for personal growth and spiritual development. This is where dealing with hardships and suffering comes in. Dr. McConnel's book provides principles that will carry us from disappointment and fear during suffering to shaping out lives with a deeper relationship with God filled with strength, courage, peace and happiness. However, we must patiently wait on God and stay in constant prayer.

Always remember to surround yourself around other Christians who can pray and give you support during hardships. You need a church family to help support you. Join with others who can pray with you, worship with you, and support you. Philippians 1:19 says "Because you are praying for me and the Spirit of Jesus Christ is helping me, I know this trouble will bring my freedom."

Dealing with hardships and suffering can impact your family members as well. So make sure you are building your family's life upon God's Word. Many of my experiences with families who buckle under the storms of life, I believe that they have not put down a firm foundation for their home. In Matthew 7, Jesus says that those who act upon His words "may be compared to a wise man who built his house on the rock. And the rain fell, and the floods came, and the winds blew and slammed against that house; and yet it did not fall, for it had been founded on the rock" (Matthew 7:24-25).

This book will provide you with the steppingstones and much needed tools to deal with hardships and sufferings knowing as a good soldier you can trust and depend on God. A miracle just may be coming your way!

Rev. Kevin L. Nelson

Contents

Introduction xiii

- **Setting the Stage:** An overview of the journey ahead, introducing the themes of faith, resilience, and the power of miracles.

Chapter 1: A Sudden Turn 1

- **The Unexpected Diagnosis:** Detailing the moment Mark received his aortic valve stenosis diagnosis and the immediate emotional impact on the family.
- **Facing Reality:** Initial reactions and the decision to lean on faith and seek medical advice.

Chapter 2: Finding Strength in Faith 9

- **Spiritual Foundation:** Exploring how faith became the cornerstone of coping with the diagnosis.
- **Scriptural Comfort:** Key scriptures that provided solace and guidance during this challenging time.
- **Building a Support System:** The role of family, friends, and church in offering emotional and spiritual support.

Chapter 3: Building a Prayer Wall 15

- **Creating a Sacred Space:** The inspiration and process behind establishing a prayer wall in the home.
- **Collective Prayers:** How the prayer wall became a focal point for community and family prayers.
- **Visualizing Faith:** The impact of having a tangible representation of prayers and hopes.

Chapter 4: Facing the Day of Surgery 36

- **Preparation and Planning:** The steps leading up to the surgery day, including medical consultations and spiritual preparations.
- **Emotional Readiness:** Managing fear and anxiety through faith and family support.
- **The Surgery Experience:** A detailed account of the surgery day, highlighting moments of trust and prayer.

Chapter 5: The Miracle of Modern Medicine 49

- **Advancements in Healthcare:** Exploring how modern medical technology contributed to Mark's successful surgery.
- **Faith Meets Medicine:** The synergy between divine intervention and medical expertise.
- **Gratitude for the Healing:** Reflecting on the gratitude felt for the medical team and God's provision.

Chapter 6: Recovery and Renewal 64

- **The Healing Process:** Mark's journey through physical recovery and the challenges faced.
- **Emotional and Spiritual Renewal:** How the experience deepened the family's faith and resilience.
- **Rebuilding Life:** Adjusting to post-surgery life and the steps taken towards complete healing.

Chapter 7: Standing Strong Together: Paris's Story 81

- **Embracing the Role of Support:** Paris shares her perspective on supporting Mark through his diagnosis and surgery.
- **Navigating Emotional Turmoil:** Managing her own fears while being a pillar of strength for the family.
- **Strengthening Family Bonds:** Efforts to maintain unity and love within the family during the crisis.
- **Building a Prayerful Home:** Integrating faith into daily life to sustain hope and resilience.
- **Leaning on Community Support:** The invaluable role of the church and community in providing assistance and prayers.
- **Personal Growth Through Adversity:** How the challenges fostered personal and spiritual growth for Paris.

- **Witnessing Miracles in Everyday Moments:** Small signs and moments that reinforced their faith.
- **A Testament of Love and Faith:** The enduring power of love and faith in overcoming life's challenges.
- **Moving Forward with Gratitude:** Continuing to live with gratitude and commitment to faith-based initiatives.

Chapter 8: Encouragement for the Waiting 93

- **Hope in Uncertainty:** Providing encouragement to readers who are waiting for their own miracles.
- **Maintaining Faith:** Strategies for keeping faith strong during periods of waiting and uncertainty.
- **Stories of Inspiration:** Sharing testimonials and stories from others who have experienced miracles through faith.

Chapter 9: A Testimony of God's Grace 110

- **Reflecting on the Journey:** Looking back on the entire experience and the lessons learned.
- **God's Unfailing Love:** Emphasizing the role of God's grace in the healing process.
- **Inspiring Others:** Encouraging readers to share their own stories of faith and miracles.

Conclusion... 119

- **Embracing the Miracle:** Summarizing the journey and the miraculous outcome through faith and medical intervention.
- **Final Encouragement:** Urging readers to trust in God and have faith in their own miracles.
- **Gratitude and Acknowledgments:** Expressing heartfelt thanks to those who supported the journey.

About the Author...121

Introduction

Almost immediately after finishing my first book, *Overcoming the Odds*, I was faced with another monumental challenge—preparing for open-heart surgery. It was as though God was saying, "You've written about overcoming challenges; now let Me take you through another so you can show others how to wait on Me for their miracle."

The news came swiftly and unexpectedly: I needed heart bypass surgery and an aortic valve replacement. It was a reality that hit hard. I had just completed sharing my journey of surviving cancer, a heart attack, and kidney failure in my first book. That story was a testament to God's faithfulness in bringing me through those trials. Yet here I was, staring down another battle, another opportunity to lean on faith, and another testimony waiting to be written.

This new journey was daunting, but I knew that God had brought me through too much to leave me now. I turned once again to Isaiah 40:31, my anchor scripture:

> "But they that wait upon the Lord shall renew their strength; they shall mount up with wings as eagles; they shall run,

and not be weary; and they shall walk,
and not faint."

This verse carried me through moments of uncertainty and fear. It reminded me that waiting for God to work is not passive—it's active. Waiting requires faith, patience, preparation, and a willingness to trust God even when the road ahead looks uncertain. I began to see this season not as a setback, but as an opportunity to draw closer to Him and to share with others the importance of trusting Him during their own waiting seasons.

The Call to Wait and Prepare

When the doctors explained the seriousness of my condition and the risks involved, I felt a familiar mixture of fear and determination. It wasn't the first time I'd been given life-altering news, but the thought of open-heart surgery was overwhelming. The weight of the decision, the risks involved, and the unknown of the recovery process loomed large in my mind.

I knew I had to prepare—not just physically, but mentally, emotionally, and spiritually. This preparation wasn't about doubting God's power to deliver me; it was about positioning myself to work alongside His plan for my healing. *James 2:26* reminds us:

> "For as the body without the spirit is
> dead, so faith without works is dead also."

I couldn't simply sit back and wait for the surgery to happen. I had to take deliberate steps to ensure the best possible outcome.

This preparation came in many forms. I followed my doctors' advice, began making dietary changes, and started focusing on ways to improve my physical health in the weeks leading up to surgery. I also sought out information about the procedure, not to fuel fear but to understand what to expect and how I could help myself recover afterward.

More than the physical preparation, I had to prepare my mind and heart for what was to come. I spent time in prayer and meditation, asking God to strengthen me and to give me peace. I leaned into His Word, finding scriptures that spoke to my situation and brought me comfort. This was a time of intentional spiritual preparation, where I reminded myself daily that God's plan is perfect, even when it's difficult to understand.

Faith in Action: Supporting My Family

One of the first things I did was consider how this journey would impact my wife and family. Almost immediately, I realized that my preparation wasn't just about me. My wife, who has been my rock and constant support throughout our marriage, would be by my side through it all. But I knew this journey would test her strength as much as mine.

I've always believed that challenges don't just affect

the person experiencing them—they ripple outward to touch everyone around them. For my wife, this meant stepping into the role of caregiver, a role she had already embraced during my earlier battles with cancer and kidney failure. I knew how heavy that responsibility could be, and I wanted to make sure she had the support she needed to navigate it.

We had honest conversations about what the coming months would look like. We talked about everything— from the logistics of hospital visits to the emotional toll of watching a loved one undergo major surgery. I encouraged her to lean on her support system, including our family, friends, and church community.

Our children and grandchildren were also a vital part of this process. I wanted them to be informed and involved, not only to support their mother but also to give them a sense of purpose during this time. As a family, we gathered together to pray, to discuss logistics, and to prepare our hearts for the journey ahead.

A Season of Prayer and Reflection

Spiritually, this was a time of deep reflection and prayer. I spent countless hours seeking God's peace and direction. Writing my first book had taught me the importance of sharing my testimony, and I realized that this next journey was another chapter in the story God was writing for my life.

I turned to scriptures that had carried me through previous trials, particularly Psalm 23:4:

> "Yea, though I walk through the valley of
> the shadow of death, I will fear no evil:
> for thou art with me; thy rod and thy staff
> they comfort me."

This verse became my daily meditation. It reminded me that I was not walking this path alone. God was with me, guiding and comforting me every step of the way. Even in the darkest moments, His presence was a source of light and peace.

Prayer became my lifeline. I prayed for strength, for wisdom, and for peace—not just for myself, but for my wife, my family, and even the medical team who would be performing the surgery. I also reached out to others for prayer, inviting my church family, close friends, and fellow pastors to intercede on my behalf. Knowing that others were lifting me up in prayer brought a profound sense of comfort and reassurance.

Learning to Wait

Philippians 4:6-7 provided immense comfort during this time:

> "Be careful for nothing; but in every
> thing by prayer and supplication with

thanksgiving let your requests be made known unto God. And the peace of God, which passeth all understanding, shall keep your hearts and minds through Christ Jesus."

Waiting is not easy. It requires patience, faith, and an active trust in God's plan. As I prepared for surgery, I realized that waiting on God didn't mean sitting idly by. It meant doing my part while trusting Him to do the rest.

Physically, I followed my doctors' recommendations and made necessary lifestyle adjustments. I focused on getting adequate rest, maintaining a positive outlook, and preparing my body for what lay ahead.

Emotionally, I reminded myself daily of God's promises. I chose to focus on His faithfulness rather than on my fears. I found strength in the testimonies of others who had walked similar journeys and come out victorious.

Spiritually, I immersed myself in God's Word. Scriptures like Philippians 4:6-7, which remind us to be anxious for nothing and to find peace in prayer, became a source of strength and encouragement.

A Word of Encouragement

Almost as soon as I finished my first book, I found myself living the next chapter of my testimony. Life often works that way. Just when we think we've overcome one obstacle, another appears. But each challenge is an opportunity to grow, to trust God more deeply, and to become a testimony for His faithfulness.

If you are reading this, I want to encourage you to see your own challenges as part of the story God is writing for your life. Waiting for a miracle is not easy, but it is an opportunity to draw closer to Him, to prepare yourself for what lies ahead, and to trust that His timing is perfect.

As I walk through this journey, I am reminded that miracles don't always happen in an instant. Sometimes, they unfold gradually, through the prayers of others, the wisdom of doctors, and the support of loved ones.

This book is written for anyone who finds themselves in a season of waiting. Whether you are waiting for healing, breakthrough, or peace, I hope my story will encourage you to hold on to faith and trust in God's plan.

Your miracle is on the way. Keep waiting, keep trusting, and keep believing.

CHAPTER 1

A Sudden Turn

*I*n September 2024, *after* returning home from our annual session of the National Baptist Convention USA, Inc., I felt unusually tired and weak. At first, I dismissed it as fatigue from the busy schedule. After all, the convention had been packed with long days, inspiring sermons, and fellowship with friends and colleagues. It wasn't unusual to feel a bit drained after such an event. But as the days went on, my body began to show signs that something was seriously wrong.

One morning, I could barely walk. Chest pain and shortness of breath followed, and I feared the worst—surely, I was having a second heart attack. My mind raced back to the first heart attack I'd experienced years ago, and I couldn't help but feel a sense of dread. Still, I knew I needed to act quickly, so I went to the emergency room.

In the emergency room, I was overwhelmed with worry but determined to trust God through it all. The doctors quickly performed blood work and discovered that I wasn't having a heart attack. Instead, they found that my hemoglobin levels were dangerously low. Something was causing me to lose blood. The initial relief of not having a heart attack was quickly overshadowed by the urgency to find the source of the bleeding.

After a series of tests, the doctors discovered a gastrointestinal (GI) bleed in my upper intestines, near the duodenum. To address it, they performed an endoscopy, threading a scope through my throat to locate and cap the bleed. They also gave me a blood transfusion to stabilize my hemoglobin levels. For a moment, it seemed the crisis had been averted.

The next morning, however, the situation worsened. Blood work revealed that the bleeding hadn't stopped. Once again, the doctors performed an endoscopy, gave me more blood, and worked to control the bleeding. What followed was a grueling three-week hospital stay, during which I underwent 12 blood transfusions and five endoscopy procedures.

Each day in the hospital brought new challenges. The physical toll of the bleeding and the repeated procedures was exhausting. I could feel my body growing weaker, and I began to wonder how much more I could endure. Yet, even in those moments, I found strength in prayer. I would lie in the hospital bed, reciting scriptures and asking God for healing. One verse that often came to mind was Psalm 46:1:

> *"God is our refuge and strength, a very present help in trouble."*

This verse reminded me that even in the midst of this trial, God was with me. He was my refuge, my strength, and my help.

Eventually, the doctors diagnosed me with Heyde's Syndrome, a condition caused by a rare defect called arteriovenous malformation (AVM). This is a congenital issue—a malformation of blood vessels in the intestines. Combined with my long-standing diagnosis of aortic valve stenosis, the AVM was causing recurrent gastrointestinal bleeds.

The doctors explained that to stop the bleeding permanently, I would need an aortic valve replacement. I had known about my aortic stenosis for years, but now it was no longer something I could delay addressing.

A Path Toward Open-Heart Surgery

During my hospital stay, my doctors suggested a procedure called TAVR (transcatheter aortic valve replacement) as a potential solution to my heart valve problem. TAVR is a less invasive procedure where the replacement valve is inserted through a catheter in the groin and guided to the heart. I was relieved by the possibility of avoiding open-heart surgery and prayed for TAVR to be an option.

The doctors explained that before they could proceed with the TAVR, they needed to perform a heart catheterization to assess the condition of my arteries. That's when the situation took a drastic turn. The heart catheterization revealed that I had severe blockages in all three of my main coronary arteries. The blockages ranged from 80% to 95%.

My hope for a simpler procedure like TAVR or even stents to clear the blockages quickly faded. The heart surgeon explained that my blockages were too severe for stents to be effective. Open-heart surgery was my only option.

When he told me, fear gripped my heart. I felt an overwhelming wave of helplessness, and tears began to flow uncontrollably. I cried like a baby, not just out of fear of the surgery but from the sheer weight of everything I had already been through. My mind raced with questions: "Why now? Why this? Haven't I faced enough?"

Yet, in the midst of that fear, I clung to one truth: God would send me a miracle. I didn't know how or when, but I believed that He would see me through the open-heart surgery. That belief became my anchor in the storm.

A Test of Faith

In that hospital room, I found myself at a crossroads of faith. On one hand, the reality of my condition and the risks of surgery were overwhelming. On the other hand, I had seen God's hand in my life before—time and time again. I knew He was faithful, and I had to trust Him to bring me through once more.

This wasn't just a physical battle; it was spiritual as well. The enemy tried to fill my mind with fear and doubt, whispering lies about what could go wrong. But God reminded me of His promises, and I leaned on scriptures that had carried me through previous trials. One verse that spoke to me deeply during this time was 2 Timothy 1:7:

> *"For God hath not given us the spirit of fear; but of power, and of love, and of a sound mind."*

Fear might have gripped me initially, but it didn't have the final say. Slowly, I began to focus on God's power and His ability to do what seemed impossible.

I also thought about my family. I couldn't let fear paralyze me because they were depending on me to fight. My wife, my children, my grandchildren, and my church family—all of them needed me to hold on to faith and trust God for the miracle we all believed was coming.

Preparing for the Journey

The days leading up to the surgery were filled with prayer, reflection, and preparation. I worked with my medical team to understand the procedure and what to expect during recovery. I spoke with my wife about how we would navigate the months ahead, and I reached out to my family, friends, and church for prayer and support.

One thing that sustained me during this time was the outpouring of love and encouragement from those around me. I received countless messages, phone calls, and prayers from people who reminded me that I wasn't alone. Their words of faith and hope lifted my spirit and reminded me of God's faithfulness.

Even in the face of uncertainty, I began to see glimpses of God's provision. The timing of my diagnosis, the skill of my doctors, and the support of my loved ones all pointed to His hand at work. Each of these moments was a reminder that He was with me, guiding me every step of the way.

As my family and I prayed, we focused on one central theme: that God's will would be done and that He would grant me the strength to face whatever lay ahead. There were moments of doubt and fear, but those moments were always overshadowed by God's peace. Philippians 4:6-7 became a source of strength for me:

> *"Be careful for nothing; but in every thing by prayer and supplication with*

thanksgiving let your requests be made known unto God. And the peace of God, which passeth all understanding, shall keep your hearts and minds through Christ Jesus."

Trusting God for the Miracle

As the day of my surgery approached, I made a conscious decision to put my trust in God. I didn't know what the outcome would be, but I believed that He was in control. I reminded myself of His promises and declared that I would walk through this trial with faith, knowing that He had a plan for my life.

The thought of open-heart surgery was still daunting, but my focus shifted from fear to faith. I began to see the surgery not as an end, but as a new beginning—a chance for God to do something extraordinary in my life.

Through it all, one thing remained constant: my belief that God would bring me through. I didn't just hope for a miracle—I expected one. And that expectation gave me the strength to face the days ahead with courage and confidence.

Closing Reflection

Looking back on those early days of my diagnosis and hospital stay, I can see how God was preparing me for what lay ahead. Every test, every procedure, and every moment of uncertainty was part of His plan to position me for healing.

I won't pretend that it was easy. There were moments of fear, doubt, and exhaustion. But through it all, God was faithful. He reminded me that He is a God of miracles, and He is able to do exceeding abundantly above all that we ask or think (Ephesians 3:20):

> *"Now unto him that is able to do exceeding*
> *abundantly above all that we ask or think,*
> *according to the power that worketh in us."*

As I prepared for open-heart surgery, I held on to that truth with everything I had. And even now, as I reflect on the journey, I am reminded that God's miracles often come in the most unexpected ways.

CHAPTER 2

Finding Strength in Faith

ollowing the harrowing experience detailed in **Chapter 1: A Sudden Turn**, the days that followed were a whirlwind of emotions, medical consultations, and soul-searching. The initial shock of my diagnosis slowly began to give way to a profound need for strength and guidance. It was during this tumultuous period that I turned deeper into my faith, seeking solace and direction from the very foundation of my beliefs.

Embracing the Journey Ahead

As the reality of my condition settled in, I realized that this journey would not be one I could navigate alone. The weight of impending surgery and the uncertainty of my health demanded more than just medical intervention; it required spiritual fortitude. I found myself reflecting on the words of Isaiah 40:31:

> *"But they that wait upon the Lord shall renew their strength; they shall mount up with wings as eagles; they shall run, and not be weary; and they shall walk, and not faint."*

This scripture became a beacon of hope, reminding me that my strength would be renewed through my reliance on God. Embracing this promise, I began to actively seek ways to fortify my spirit and prepare myself for the challenges ahead.

Seeking Community Support

Understanding the importance of community, I reached out to my church family and close friends for support. Their unwavering faith and willingness to stand by me provided a much-needed sense of comfort and assurance. We organized regular prayer meetings, both at home and within the church, creating a network of intercessors dedicated to my healing journey.

During one particularly moving prayer session, one preacher shared a passage that resonated deeply with me. Proverbs 18:10 states:

*"The name of the Lord is a strong tower:
the righteous runneth into it, and is safe."*

These gatherings became a sanctuary where fears were expressed, prayers were lifted, and faith was collectively strengthened. The solidarity of my community underscored the belief that we are stronger together, united in purpose and prayer.

Initiating Spiritual Practices

In the midst of medical appointments and preparations, I sought to establish spiritual practices that would sustain me throughout my ordeal. Daily devotionals became a cornerstone of my routine, allowing me to center my thoughts on God's promises and teachings. One morning, as I meditated on Psalm 23:4, I felt a profound sense of peace:

"Yea, though I walk through the valley of the shadow of death, I will fear no evil: for thou art with me; thy rod and thy staff they comfort me."

This verse provided immense comfort, assuring me of God's perpetual presence, even in the darkest times. Incorporating such scriptures into my daily life helped shift my focus from fear to faith, reinforcing the belief that I was not alone in this journey.

Planning for the Miracle

With the date of my surgery approaching, I knew that preparation was paramount—not just physically, but spiritually and emotionally as well. I began to envision the creation of a prayer wall, a tangible representation of the prayers and faith that surrounded me. This concept, inspired by my desire to visualize collective support, would later be elaborated upon in **Chapter 3: Building a Prayer Wall.**

In anticipation of this, I started gathering materials and involving my family in the process. The act of creating the prayer wall became a collective endeavor, symbolizing our united faith and hope for my healing. Each prayer note, scripture verse, and affirmation added to the wall served as a testament to the power of community and divine intervention.

Reflecting on Personal Growth

Throughout this preparatory phase, I found myself undergoing significant personal growth. The challenges posed by my health condition prompted a deeper introspection into my faith and purpose. Romans 5:3-4 became a guiding light during moments of frustration and despair:

> *"And not only so, but we glory in tribulations also: knowing that tribulation worketh*

*patience; And patience, experience; and
experience, hope."*

This passage reinforced the notion that trials were not merely obstacles but opportunities for spiritual maturation and the cultivation of unwavering hope. Embracing this perspective allowed me to navigate the uncertainties with a resilient spirit, trusting that each step was part of a divine plan.

Preparing My Family for the Journey

Recognizing the emotional toll this journey would take on my loved ones, I made it a priority to prepare them for the road ahead. Open and honest conversations about my fears, hopes, and expectations fostered a supportive environment where everyone felt empowered to express their emotions and contribute to my healing process.

Ephesians 4:2-3 encapsulated my approach to these discussions:

> *"With all lowliness and meekness, with
> longsuffering, forbearing one another in
> love; Endeavouring to keep the unity of
> the Spirit in the bond of peace."*

By embodying these virtues, I aimed to create a harmonious and cohesive support system, ensuring that our collective faith remained strong and unshaken.

Anticipating the Miracle

As the days drew nearer to my surgery, a sense of anticipation filled the air. The prayer wall was nearing completion, adorned with heartfelt prayers, uplifting scriptures, and symbols of faith. It stood as a visual affirmation of the miracles we were collectively seeking, bridging the gap between our prayers and the impending medical intervention.

In the quiet moments before the surgery, I found solace in the words of Philippians 4:13:

> *"I can do all things through Christ which strengtheneth me."*

This declaration of faith became my mantra, empowering me to face the surgery with courage and unwavering trust in God's plan.

CHAPTER 3

Building a Prayer Wall

*I*mmediately after hearing the news that I needed open-heart surgery, the words of an old hymn we used to sing in church flooded my spirit:

> *"Prayer makes me strong when I am weak."*

One thing I know more than anything is prayer. The late Dr. C.A.W. Clark said, "Prayer is drawing from Divine resources." He emphasized, "Prayer is the instrument where we draw from God's inexhaustible well." In that moment, I realized just how crucial prayer was to my situation. I knew that prayer was my call to Divine resources, a lifeline that could sustain me through the challenging times ahead.

Witnessing the Power of Prayer

From a very young age, my involvement in the church provided me with a solid foundation of faith and a profound understanding of prayer's transformative power. Growing up in a close-knit congregation, I was surrounded by stories of faith, hope, and divine intervention. I witnessed firsthand how sincere prayers could alter the course of lives, bringing hope, healing, and peace in the midst of turmoil.

One of my earliest memories of prayer's impact was during a particularly hot summer. My neighbor, a widow across the street, asked me to help cut her grass. She supplied the gas and the lawnmower, trusting me with her yard care. This seemingly simple request held significant meaning for me. At that time, I had been praying earnestly for some money that I needed, unsure of where it would come from. Accepting her request felt like a response to my prayers; it was a tangible way in which God provided for my needs through the kindness of others.

This experience taught me that prayer is not just about asking for help but also about trusting in God's provision through the people He places in our lives. It reinforced the belief that prayer is a dialogue with God, where His answers can come in unexpected and often beautiful ways.

Another poignant example from my childhood occurred one day at school. I split my pants badly, an embarrassing and painful accident. At that time, the teacher would allow us to walk home to change clothes. However, the path home posed an additional challenge—three large Doberman Pinschers, known for their protective and sometimes aggressive nature, roamed freely in the neighbor's yard around the corner from our house.

I had always been afraid of dogs, especially these formidable Dobermans. The thought of encountering them while walking home filled me with anxiety and fear. I desperately wanted to find a place to hide until the owners returned to secure the dogs, but my school was exactly one mile from home, a distance I had to traverse alone.

As I walked that mile, my mind was a whirlwind of fear and uncertainty. I began praying to God for a miracle—a way to safely make it home without encountering the aggressive dogs. My faith told me to trust in God's protection and to proceed with confidence.

As I approached the street just before mine, I could see the three dogs playing in the yard. My heart raced, and I froze, contemplating what to do next. I continued to pray, seeking guidance and courage. Summoning all the faith I could muster, I began to walk past the dogs. To my astonishment, as I got closer, the dogs suddenly stopped playing. They stood alertly, watching me with intent eyes but making no move to attack. I walked right past them without incident.

This incident was a clear demonstration of God's intervention through prayer. My heartfelt plea for safety was answered in a miraculous way, reinforcing my belief in the power of prayer and divine protection. It was a poignant reminder that faith can move mountains, providing strength and courage in the face of fear and adversity.

Seeking a Miracle

As I faced the reality of open-heart surgery, I knew that I was looking for a miracle from God—a miraculous healing of my body. A miracle, to me, is an extraordinary event that defies natural laws and brings about divine intervention. It is a testament to God's power and His ability to transform lives in profound ways.

Faith is the key, and prayer unlocks the door. This belief became the cornerstone of my approach to the impending surgery. I understood that while medicine and surgery were necessary, it was my faith and prayer that would provide the strength and assurance needed to endure the process and trust in God's plan for my healing.

Establishing a Prayer Routine

In preparation for my open-heart surgery, I knew that I needed to establish a consistent prayer routine to maintain my faith and resilience. Prayer became an integral part of my daily life, offering a sense of purpose and direction amidst the uncertainty.

I began by asking my wife, Paris, our children, and grandchildren to pray for me. Their collective prayers provided a strong support system, reinforcing my faith and offering emotional comfort. I also reached out to my siblings and extended family, requesting their prayers and support during this challenging time.

Recognizing the importance of community, I turned to New Cornerstone Baptist Church, asking the congregation to pray for me. Additionally, I sought prayers from our State Convention, Baptist General State Convention of Illinois, and all my pastor friends, urging them to add my name to their churches' prayer list. The immediate and heartfelt responses from these pastors and church members were overwhelming. Their collective prayers created a continuous flow of divine support, strengthening my faith and providing the emotional strength needed to face the impending surgery.

I also reached out to as many people as I knew, asking them to pray for me. Friends, colleagues, neighbors, and even acquaintances joined in prayer, demonstrating the far-reaching impact of faith and community support. Each prayer, whether received personally or through broader church networks, added another layer of hope and assurance.

Furthermore, I asked the doctors and hospital staff at Northwestern Hospital in Chicago, Illinois, where the surgery was to take place, to pray for me. Knowing that the medical professionals involved in my care were praying for my healing provided an additional sense of comfort and trust in the hands that would be operating on my heart.

Building and Maintaining the Prayer Wall

With the support of my family, friends, and church community, I set out to create my prayer wall—a physical representation of the prayers and faith that surrounded me. The prayer wall became a central focal point in my home, a place where I could visualize the collective prayers and feel the presence of God.

I chose a large bulletin board for the prayer wall, ensuring it was easily accessible and visible. The process of organizing the prayer wall was both therapeutic and uplifting. I began by writing down my prayer requests, personal reflections, and meaningful scriptures. Each prayer request was a heartfelt plea for healing and strength, while the scriptures served as affirmations of God's promises and faithfulness.

Paris and our children assisted in setting up the prayer wall, adding their own notes of encouragement and prayers. This collaborative effort strengthened our familial bonds and created a shared space for faith and reflection. The interactive nature of the prayer wall allowed us to update it regularly, adding new prayers and removing those that had been answered or no longer needed attention.

To enhance the visual appeal and significance of the prayer wall, I incorporated various symbols and colors that held personal meaning. Each scripture verse was highlighted in a different color, making them stand out and easy to reference during prayer sessions. Inspirational quotes and testimonies of answered prayers were also included, serving as constant reminders of God's active presence in our lives.

The Power of Collective Prayer

The true strength of the prayer wall lay in the collective prayers that it represented. Knowing that a community of believers was praying for my healing provided an immense sense of peace and assurance. It was a powerful reminder that I was not alone in my struggle; I was part of a larger body of faith that stood with me in prayer.

During moments of anxiety and fear, I would turn to the prayer wall, reading the prayers and scriptures that adorned it. The collective prayers served as a source of strength, helping me to overcome moments of doubt and reinforcing my trust in God's plan. Each prayer, whether spoken aloud or silently recited, contributed to a tapestry of faith that enveloped me, providing both spiritual and emotional support.

The prayer wall also became a living journal of my

spiritual journey. As prayers were answered and new needs arose, the wall evolved, reflecting the dynamic nature of faith and healing. This tangible record of prayers and their outcomes served as ongoing encouragement, reminding me of God's faithfulness and the power of persistent prayer.

Overcoming Doubt with Faith

Despite the strong foundation of prayer, moments of doubt occasionally crept in. The severity of my condition and the uncertainty of the road ahead sometimes made me question whether a miracle was possible. During these challenging times, I leaned even harder into prayer and scripture, seeking reassurance and reaffirming my trust in God.

One particularly challenging night, overwhelmed by fear, I turned to **Psalm 34:4**:

> *"I sought the LORD, and he heard me,*
> *and delivered me out of all my fears."*

Reciting this verse, I felt a renewed sense of hope and strength. It was a reminder that God hears my prayers and is with me in every moment of fear and doubt. This reliance on scripture and prayer helped me navigate the emotional turmoil, keeping me anchored in faith.

Additionally, meditating on **Romans 8:28**—*"And we know that all things work together for good to them* *that love God, to them who are the called according to his purpose."*—provided a broader perspective on my suffering. It reinforced the belief that every trial was part of a divine plan, leading to a greater purpose beyond my immediate understanding.

During moments of doubt, I found solace in the stories of biblical figures who faced immense challenges yet remained steadfast in their faith. The resilience of Job, the unwavering trust of Abraham, and the courage of Daniel served as blueprints for maintaining faith amidst adversity. These reflections not only dispelled my doubts but also reinforced my commitment to persevere through prayer and trust in God's unwavering love.

Job's unwavering faith despite his suffering taught me the importance of maintaining trust in God even when circumstances seem bleak. Abraham's journey of faith, marked by trials and promises, reminded me that God's plans are greater than our own and that His timing is perfect. Daniel's courage in the face of persecution inspired me to stand firm in my beliefs, knowing that God is always by my side.

These biblical examples provided a framework for understanding my own struggles, helping me to see them as opportunities for growth and deeper reliance on God. They reinforced the notion that faith is not the absence of doubt but the strength to overcome it through prayer and trust in God's unwavering love.

The Role of Faith in Healing

Throughout this journey, faith played an integral role in my healing process. It wasn't just about physical recovery but also about spiritual growth and transformation. Building a prayer wall was a manifestation of my faith—a tangible expression of my trust in God's ability to work miracles.

Faith gave me the resilience to endure the grueling hospital stay, the repeated procedures, and the overwhelming uncertainty. It provided a sense of purpose and direction, guiding me through the darkest moments and illuminating the path toward healing. Each day, as I engaged in prayer and reflected on scripture, my faith grew stronger, fortifying my spirit against the challenges I faced.

Moreover, faith transformed my perspective on suffering and challenges. Instead of viewing them as mere obstacles, I began to see them as opportunities for growth and deeper reliance on God. This shift in mindset was crucial in maintaining my hope and determination throughout the ordeal. It allowed me to approach each day with a sense of purpose, knowing that my struggles were part of a larger divine plan.

I started to engage in deeper spiritual practices, such as extended periods of prayer and meditation, to seek a closer connection with God. These practices not only strengthened my spirit but also enhanced my mental and emotional well-being, contributing to a holistic healing process. The more I immersed myself in prayer, the more I felt a profound sense of peace and assurance, even in the face of uncertainty.

Faith also brought clarity to my thoughts and emotions. It helped me to prioritize what truly mattered, focusing on gratitude, love, and hope rather than fear and despair. This emotional resilience was essential in navigating the ups and downs of my health journey, allowing me to remain steadfast and optimistic despite the challenges.

Encouraging Others to Build Their Own Prayer Walls

As I reflect on my experience, I realize the profound impact that building a prayer wall can have on one's journey of faith. It's not just a personal practice but a communal one, bringing people together in a unified act of intercession and support.

For those who find themselves waiting for a miracle, I encourage you to build your own prayer wall. Start with personal prayer, inviting others to join you in intercession. Let your prayer wall be a source of strength, hope, and faith, guiding you through your trials and leading you toward God's miraculous intervention.

One of the most rewarding aspects of building my prayer wall was witnessing its impact on others. Friends and family members became inspired to create their own prayer walls, sharing their needs and interceding for one another. It fostered a sense of unity and mutual support, strengthening our collective faith.

I encouraged others to build their own prayer walls by sharing my experience and offering guidance on how to start. Seeing others embrace this practice reinforced the power of prayer and community in our lives. It was a beautiful cycle of faith—one prayer wall leading to another, each one a testament to God's unwavering love and provision.

For example, one young woman that I Knew Mary, was going through a difficult divorce. After hearing about my prayer wall, she decided to create her own, inviting her friends and church members to intercede on her behalf. Over time, she experienced moments of clarity and peace that she attributes to the collective prayers surrounding her. Her story became another testament to the transformative power of prayer walls, inspiring others in similar situations to seek divine intervention through collective faith.

Another inspiring example came from my neighbor, Tom, who was battling a chronic illness. He felt overwhelmed by the daily struggles and feared that his condition would never improve. After seeing the impact of my prayer wall, he decided to start his own, inviting his family, friends, and church members to pray for his healing. As he witnessed the unwavering support and the continuous prayers, Tom began to feel a renewed sense of hope and strength. His faith deepened, and he started to perceive subtle improvements in his health, which he confidently attributes to the power of collective prayer.

These examples illustrate how building a prayer wall can create a ripple effect of faith and support, extending beyond individual experiences to uplift entire communities. It fosters a culture of intercession, where believers stand together in prayer, supporting one another through life's most challenging moments.

Practical Steps to Build Your Prayer Wall

Here are some practical steps to help you build your own prayer wall:

Create a Prayer Journal:

- **Document Your Prayers:** Write down your prayers, the prayers of others, and the ways God answers them. This journal serves as a tangible record of your spiritual journey.
- **Reflect on Your Journey:** Use the journal to reflect on your experiences, noting how prayer has impacted your life and contributed to your healing.

Organize Prayer Meetings:

- **Schedule Regular Meetings:** Set aside time each week for prayer meetings with family, friends, and church members. Consistent prayer meetings foster a sense of community and shared faith.

- **Share Your Needs:** Use these meetings to share your prayer requests and listen to the needs of others. This mutual support strengthens the bonds within the group.

Develop a Prayer Routine:

- **Establish Daily Rituals:** Incorporate prayer into your daily routine by setting aside specific times for prayer, such as morning devotionals and evening reflections.
- **Use Reminders:** Utilize visual or auditory reminders, like setting alarms or placing scripture verses around your home, to prompt regular prayer.

Use Visual Reminders:

- **Create a Physical Prayer Wall:** Set up a bulletin board or wall space in your home where you can post prayer requests, scriptures, and testimonies of answered prayers.
- **Interactive Elements:** Use sticky notes, pins, or magnets to add and update prayers easily. This interactive aspect makes the prayer wall a dynamic and evolving testament to your faith journey.

Engage in Corporate Prayer:

- **Participate in Church Prayers:** Actively engage in corporate prayer sessions at your church. These collective prayers amplify the power of intercession and unify the congregation.
- **Encourage Group Prayer:** Motivate others in your community to include your prayer needs in their prayers, fostering a network of support.

Pray with Scripture:

- **Align Prayers with God's Word:** Use specific scriptures as the basis for your prayers, aligning your requests with God's promises and declarations.
- **Meditate on Verses:** Spend time meditating on selected verses during prayer, allowing them to shape your petitions and reinforce your faith.

Express Gratitude:

- **Thank God for Prayers:** Regularly express gratitude to God for the prayers and support you receive. Acknowledging His faithfulness helps maintain a positive and hopeful outlook.
- **Appreciate Supporters:** Show appreciation to those who intercede on your behalf, strengthening your relationships and encouraging continued support.

Share Testimonies:

- **Celebrate Answered Prayers:** Share stories of answered prayers with your prayer group and church community. These testimonies inspire faith and demonstrate God's active presence in your life.

- **Encourage Others:** Encourage others to share their testimonies, fostering an environment of mutual encouragement and faith reinforcement.

By systematically implementing these steps, the prayer wall becomes an integral part of your daily life, providing both spiritual nourishment and tangible evidence of God's active presence in your healing journey.

Prayer Wall as a Lifelong Practice

Building a prayer wall was not just a temporary measure during my time of need; it became a lifelong practice that continues to enrich my faith journey. While the surgery was on the horizon, the prayer wall had already ingrained itself as a central part of my spiritual routine. This preparedness meant that as I approached the surgery, I was already equipped with a strong foundation of prayer and community support. The prayer wall provided a sense of continuity and stability, ensuring that my faith remained unwavering as I faced the unknown.

Integrating the prayer wall into daily life meant that

prayer became an integral part of every routine. Whether I was facing minor inconveniences or major life decisions, the prayer wall served as a constant source of guidance and strength. It reminded me to seek divine wisdom in all circumstances, fostering a habit of continual communication with God.

Moreover, the prayer wall was poised to evolve beyond my personal needs. As I prepared for surgery, I began to include prayers for the medical team, my family, and others who were part of my journey. This expansion highlighted the comprehensive nature of prayer, addressing not just personal concerns but also the broader needs of those around us.

Legacy of Prayer:

The prayer wall also became a legacy that I intended to pass on to my family and congregation. I planned to teach my children and church members the importance of prayer and how to build their own prayer walls. This legacy ensured that the power of prayer would continue to uplift and support not just me but also those around me.

Teaching others to build their own prayer walls would create a ripple effect of faith within my community. It would encourage a culture of intercession and mutual support, where everyone felt empowered to seek and offer prayers. This collective faith journey would strengthen the bonds within our community, making us more resilient in the face of challenges.

Additionally, the prayer wall became a tool for mentoring younger members of the congregation. By guiding them through the process of building their own prayer walls, I helped instill the importance of prayer and communal support from an early age. This mentorship ensured that the practice of collective prayer would be carried forward by future generations, maintaining its vital role in our community.

Moreover, maintaining a prayer wall fostered a deeper sense of gratitude and awareness of God's presence in my daily life. It encouraged me to remain vigilant in my prayers, not just during times of crisis but as a continuous practice of faith and devotion. This persistent focus on prayer enhanced my spiritual growth, making faith an ever-present aspect of my existence.

Strength Through Community Support

The support from my community was instrumental in sustaining my faith. My wife, Paris, friends, and church members not only prayed for me but also provided practical assistance—helping with household tasks, bringing meals, and offering a listening ear. Their actions demonstrated the love of Christ in tangible ways, reinforcing the prayers that were lifting me up.

During one of my hospital visits, a group of church members organized a prayer meeting. Additionally, volunteers from the church took on various tasks to support my family, ensuring that my wife and children had the assistance they needed. This practical help alleviated some of the burdens we faced, allowing us to focus more on prayer and faith.

These acts of service and love were a living testament to the teachings of Christ, embodying the essence of community and mutual support. They provided not only physical relief but also emotional and spiritual encouragement, fortifying my resolve to trust in God's plan.

Furthermore, the emotional support from church members played a significant role in my healing process. Sharing my fears and hopes with them provided a safe space to express my vulnerabilities. Their empathetic listening and affirming words fortified my spirit, reminding me that I was surrounded by a loving and supportive community.

The Evolution of My Prayer Wall

Over time, my prayer wall evolved into a dynamic and interactive part of my healing journey. It wasn't just a static list of prayers but a living testament to God's ongoing work in my life. Each prayer added to the wall was a building block in the ever-growing fortress of faith that surrounded me.

I began to see the prayer wall as a reflection of my relationship with God. It was a visual representation of my trust, my reliance on His promises, and my commitment to seeking Him in every circumstance. The wall became a source of inspiration, reminding me daily of the prayers that surrounded me and the faith that sustained me.

As my health journey progressed, the prayer wall expanded to include prayers for others, fostering a spirit of generosity and intercession. This shift from a personal to a communal focus enriched my prayer life, allowing me to support others as I had been supported.

The evolution of the prayer wall also mirrored my personal growth. Initially, it was a symbol of my need and vulnerability, but as it grew, it became a testament to my faith and resilience. Each new prayer added to the wall was not just a request but a declaration of faith, an affirmation that I believed in God's ability to heal and restore.

Moreover, the prayer wall became a tool for tracking my spiritual and emotional progress. By noting the prayers I had made and the prayers of others who were lifting me up, I could see the ways in which God was working in my life. This tangible record provided ongoing encouragement, especially during moments when uncertainty loomed large.

Another aspect of the prayer wall's evolution was its integration into daily family life. My children and grandchildren became involved in adding their own prayer requests and blessings, teaching them the importance of prayer from a young age. This family-oriented approach ensured that the prayer wall was a shared experience, strengthening our familial bonds and our collective faith.

As my life returned to a semblance of normalcy, the prayer wall continued to serve as a constant reminder of the trials I had faced and the faith that had sustained me. It became a symbol of resilience, a visual testament to the power of prayer and community support in overcoming life's greatest challenges.

Conclusion

Building a prayer wall was a transformative experience that reinforced my faith and connected me with a supportive community. It was a tangible expression of my trust in God and a testament to the power of collective prayer. As I continued to wait on my miracle, the prayer wall remained a steadfast source of strength and hope, reminding me that I was never alone in my journey.

Prayer truly makes us strong when we are weak. It is the foundation upon which we build our faith and the key to unlocking God's miraculous intervention in our lives. As you embark on your own journey of waiting, consider building your own prayer wall. Let it be a source of strength, a symbol of your faith, and a testament to God's enduring love and power.

CHAPTER 4
Facing the Day of Surgery

*B*y the time the day of surgery arrived, I felt the unmistakable presence of the Holy Spirit as my comforter. The Bible verse that echoed in my heart was John 14:27:

> *"Peace I leave with you, my peace I give unto you: not as the world giveth, give I unto you. Let not your heart be troubled, neither let it be afraid."*

This verse became my anchor, grounding me in a perfect peace that surpassed all understanding. I was in a good mental space because I had the unwavering expectation that God was orchestrating my miracle. Instead of fear, I felt a profound sense of happiness and anticipation for what was about to unfold.

Overwhelming Peace and Family Support

I experienced overwhelming peace prior to surgery because my mind was stayed on Jesus. My prayer wall, built strong throughout the Christian community, helped anchor me in hope and peace. My children all kept reassuring me that everything would be alright. My two grandsons, Jayden (7) and Jordan (4), understood that granddad was sick but would come to me sometimes together and give me a hug, and I would hold them real tight. I found great strength in that.

Their innocent hugs were more than just physical comfort; they were spiritual affirmations of love and faith. Watching their simple trust in me reinforced my own trust in God. Their presence reminded me that my battle was not just my own but also for the generations to come. Each hug from Jayden and Jordan was a silent prayer, a gesture that spoke volumes about faith and resilience.

The day of the surgery was an opportunity for me to demonstrate faith in God to our family. I did not want them to see me demonstrating fear or anxiety but complete trust in God. I also saw this as me—a husband, father, and grandfather—giving leadership to our family. Additionally, it was a way to teach faith and trust in God to our church and the Christian community.

Dr. Mark and Paris McConnell

The Core Support Group

I was blessed with the unwavering support of my wife, Paris, our three sons, Moses, Caleb, and Matthew, two grandsons, Jayden and Jordan, daughter-in-law Alicia, and our church administrator and her husband Lorita and James Taylor. My cousin Cleaster and her husband Cliff. This core group of my family traveled with me to Northwestern Hospital in Chicago, Illinois. Their presence was a source of immense strength and comfort. Additionally, my brothers, sisters, uncles, aunts, cousins, and countless others joined in supporting me, each offering prayers, encouragement, and practical assistance.

Paris, my wife, has been my rock through every storm. Her unwavering faith and practical support have been indispensable. Moses, Caleb, and Matthew, our sons, have each demonstrated their own unique ways of showing support—whether through prayer, comforting words, or taking on additional responsibilities at home. Alicia, our daughter-in-law, managed logistics and ensured that everything was in place for the day ahead. Lorita and James Taylor, our church administrator and her husband, provided both spiritual and emotional support, reinforcing the sense of community that enveloped me.

The Journey to Chicago

On Sunday, the day before my open-heart surgery, our core group traveled by train from Peoria, Illinois, to

38

Chicago. The journey was more than just a physical trip; it was a spiritual pilgrimage filled with faith and anticipation. We arrived at Northwestern Hospital with a shared sense of purpose and hope.

As the train chugged along, I took moments to reflect on the support system surrounding me. Each face around me was a reminder of the collective faith that was holding me up. Conversations were filled with affirmations of God's goodness and prayers for my successful surgery. The rhythmic sound of the train became a backdrop to my thoughts, each mile bringing me closer to the moment where my faith would be put to the ultimate test.

That evening, at 5:00 p.m., we gathered for a wonderful dinner. It was an opportunity for me to express my complete faith in God and to thank everyone for their prayers and support. The meal was not just a routine gathering; it transformed into a time of worship and communal anticipation. We sang hymns, shared testimonies of faith, and collectively awaited the miracle God was about to perform in my life.

The dinner table was adorned with symbols of faith—candles flickered softly, casting a warm glow, and scripture verses were displayed prominently. As we dined, the conversations naturally shifted to prayers and blessings for the day ahead. The atmosphere was thick with expectancy, each prayer uttered a thread weaving us closer together in faith.

Morning of the Surgery

When I woke up early the next day, I felt energized and calm. The surgery was scheduled for 7:30 a.m., and I knew it was time to place my trust fully in God. At 5:30 a.m., we checked into the hospital, and the preparations for surgery began.

My wife had helped me arrange a playlist of uplifting and worship songs on my phone, which I played continuously during registration and preparation. These songs filled the air with faith and hope, creating an atmosphere of divine presence. As the medical team prepared me for surgery, I focused my mind on God and His Word, reciting scriptures that fortified my faith.

The hospital environment was serene; the halls were quiet, and the air was filled with the soft hum of medical equipment and hushed conversations. Despite the many people checking in for their surgeries that day, there was a palpable sense of calmness, as if faith itself was a guiding force present in every room.

The Power of Prayer and Community

A dear friend of mine, Pastor Claude White from Peoria, Illinois, came to be with me, along with Pastor Craig Smith from Chicago, Illinois, and my cousin, Darrell Horn. Together, we prayed fervently, seeking God's guidance and protection. Their prayers were a testament to the power of collective faith, providing me with immense spiritual and emotional support.

The environment at the hospital was serene; there were many people checking in for their surgeries that day. I spoke to a young woman who was having a tumor resection. She was very nervous, so I shared the scripture that says, "God can do exceedingly abundantly above all that we can ask or think" (Ephesians 3:20). I asked her if I might lead her in prayer. She began to cry, and I encouraged her to trust God's plan for her life. She cried even more and thanked me for putting Christ before her surgery. This interaction reinforced the profound impact of faith and prayer, not only on my own journey but also on those around me.

The young woman's response was a poignant reminder that faith is contagious. Her tears were not just of fear but of the profound relief and comfort that comes from placing trust in God. This encounter underscored the ripple effect of shared faith and how it can transform fear into peace.

A Moment of Reassurance

As I woke up from surgery, my cousin Cleaster and her husband began talking to me. Cleaster is a former heart surgeon. She said, "Good job, cousin. I knew you could do it." Having her talk to me really helped to keep me calm. I had a respiratory tube down my throat and was unable to talk back. I heard her say that the surgery took seven hours. She said, "I'm proud of you. Stay calm; they are coming to take the tube in your throat." All I could do in my spirit was praise God. I knew that it was no one but the Lord. They removed the tube from my throat early the next morning. I did start right then to feel better.

Cleaster's words of encouragement were a profound reassurance during a vulnerable moment. Her presence and expertise provided both emotional and spiritual comfort, reinforcing my trust in God's plan and the capabilities of the medical team. Even though I couldn't respond verbally, her words resonated deeply within me, serving as a bridge between my internal peace and the external support system.

Trusting God's Plan

In that moment, I fully embraced the truth of Proverbs 3:5-6:

> *"Trust in the Lord with all your heart and lean not on your own understanding; in all your ways submit to him, and he will make your paths straight."*

This scripture resonated deeply as I prepared to undergo surgery. I understood that while I was taking the necessary physical steps towards healing, it was my faith that was truly guiding me through this trial.

Reflecting on this verse, I realized that my trust in God was not a passive act but an active commitment to surrender every aspect of my life to Him. It was a declaration that no matter how complex or daunting the situation, God's wisdom and plan were paramount. This understanding fortified my spirit, allowing me to face the surgery with unwavering confidence.

The Surgical Procedure

As I lay on the operating table, surrounded by the prayers and support of my loved ones, I felt a profound sense of peace. The medical team moved with precision and care, each action a reflection of their expertise and dedication. I trusted in their skills, knowing that God was working through them to bring about my healing.

The surgery was intense and demanding, but my heart was at ease. I knew that God was with me every step of the way, guiding the surgeons, the nurses, and every member of the medical staff involved in my care. The sterile environment of the operating room became a sanctuary of faith, where the divine and the medical seamlessly intertwined.

Throughout the seven-hour procedure, I remained in a state of deep prayer and meditation. Visualizing the prayer wall and the collective prayers from my community helped sustain my focus on God's promises. Even in the midst of the physical challenges, my spiritual fortitude remained unshaken, a testament to the profound connection between faith and healing.

Awakening with Hope

When I began to awaken from the surgery, I felt a renewed sense of hope and gratitude. The prayers of my family, friends, and church community had enveloped me, and I could feel the tangible presence of God in my recovery. My mind was filled with peace, and I knew that my miracle was unfolding as I had faithfully anticipated.

The first moments of awakening were disorienting, but the comforting presence of my loved ones and the lingering sense of God's peace guided me through the initial confusion. Cleaster's reassuring words echoed in my mind, reminding me that I was not alone and that God had indeed blessed me with the expertise and compassion of the medical team.

Reflecting on the Experience

Looking back on that day, I realize how pivotal it was in my faith journey. Facing open-heart surgery was one of the most challenging moments of my life, yet it became a profound testament to the power of prayer and the importance of community support. The experience deepened my relationship with God and reinforced my belief in His ability to perform miracles.

Each moment of the surgery was a lesson in trust and

surrender. I learned that true peace comes not from the absence of fear but from the presence of God. The support of my family and church community demonstrated the tangible ways in which faith can manifest through collective action and unwavering belief.

Moving Forward with Gratitude

As I continue to recover, I carry with me the lessons learned from this journey. The unwavering support of my family and church, the power of collective prayer, and the peace that comes from trusting in God's plan have become integral parts of my daily life. I am more committed than ever to sharing my testimony, hoping to inspire others to hold on to faith during their own seasons of waiting.

The journey did not end with the surgery; it evolved into a path of healing and continued faith. Each day brought new challenges and opportunities to grow spiritually and emotionally. The gratitude I feel extends beyond my immediate family to the broader Christian community that stood with me in prayer and support.

Embracing a New Beginning

The aftermath of the surgery marked the beginning of a new chapter in my life. Recovery was gradual, with each small improvement serving as a testament to God's enduring presence and the effectiveness of modern medicine guided by faith. Physical healing was accompanied by spiritual growth, as I delved deeper into prayer and reflection, understanding the intricate ways in which faith and health are interconnected.

During my recovery, I took time to revisit the prayer wall, adding new prayers for continued healing and gratitude for the progress made. The wall became a living testament to God's work in my life, each prayer a step towards complete restoration. It also became a focal point for my family, a place where we could collectively offer thanks and seek further blessings.

Strengthening Faith Through Adversity

This experience reinforced the concept that faith is not the absence of doubt but the ability to overcome it through unwavering trust in God. The challenges I faced during and after the surgery served as catalysts for deeper spiritual understanding and resilience. Each prayer, each moment of reflection, and each act of support from my loved ones strengthened my resolve to maintain a steadfast faith, regardless of the circumstances.

I began to see my story not just as a personal journey but as a narrative that could inspire and uplift others. The lessons learned from this experience became valuable teachings for our family and church community, demonstrating the profound impact of faith-driven support systems in times of crisis.

The Role of Gratitude in Healing

Gratitude played a crucial role in my healing process. Acknowledging the blessings in my life, from the support of my family to the skilled hands of my medical team, shifted my focus from fear to thankfulness. Each day, I made it a point to express gratitude through prayer, journaling, and sharing heartfelt thanks with those who stood by me.

This practice of gratitude not only enhanced my emotional well-being but also deepened my connection with God. It reminded me that even in the darkest moments, there are countless reasons to be thankful, reinforcing the belief that God's plans are always for our ultimate good.

Sharing the Miracle

As I regained my strength, I felt a compelling desire to share my story more broadly. The miracle of my healing was not just a personal victory but a divine testimony meant to inspire others. I began to document my experiences, intending to use them as a foundation for future chapters in this book. Each reflection, each prayer, and each moment of support became a piece of a larger narrative aimed at encouraging others to trust in God's plan during their own trials.

The interactions I had during the surgery day, like leading the young woman in prayer, reinforced the importance of sharing faith in actionable ways. It became clear that my journey was intertwined with the faith journeys of those around me, creating a network of shared hope and divine intervention.

CHAPTER 5

The Miracle of Modern Medicine

M odern medicine has truly come a long way, transforming from rudimentary procedures to sophisticated, life-saving interventions that were once unimaginable. This chapter explores the profound advancements in medical science through the lens of my family's personal experiences with heart disease, highlighting how these developments have been nothing short of miraculous.

A Legacy of Heart Disease

My journey with heart disease began with my father in 1990. He was diagnosed with heart disease, and the procedure chosen for him was an angioplasty, commonly referred to as "the balloon." At that time, angioplasty was a groundbreaking procedure aimed at widening narrowed or blocked arteries to improve blood flow to the heart. However, the technology was still in its early stages. During my father's angioplasty surgery, complications arose when his heart went into fibrillation—a severe and life-threatening irregular heartbeat. Despite the doctors' best efforts, they were unable to stabilize him, and he tragically passed away on the operating table.

Our family is deeply rooted in Christian faith, and throughout this heartbreaking experience, we placed our trust in God. We believed that His will was paramount, and while we grappled with our loss, our faith provided us with strength and hope.

A New Generation Faces Heart Disease

Fast forward 34 years, and the tables turned. As the oldest son, I found myself facing the same battle with heart disease. Unlike my father's experience, medical science had made significant strides by the time it was my turn to seek treatment. At 61, I was diagnosed with severe blockages in all three main arteries, accompanied by aortic valve stenosis—a condition where the valve between the heart and the aorta narrows, impeding blood flow.

The doctors recommended open-heart surgery, specifically a quadruple bypass. This procedure involves creating new pathways for blood to flow around the blocked arteries, thereby restoring adequate blood supply to the heart muscle. Additionally, addressing the aortic valve stenosis required valve replacement, and I received a biodegradable aortic repair. This advanced procedure not only repaired the valve but also utilized biodegradable materials that reduce the risk of long-term complications and promote natural healing.

The Significance of Open-Heart Surgery and Bypass Techniques

Open-heart surgery represents one of the pinnacles of modern surgical achievement. Unlike less invasive procedures, open-heart surgery allows surgeons direct access to the heart and its major vessels, enabling comprehensive treatment of complex heart conditions. The quadruple bypass I underwent involved grafting healthy blood vessels from other parts of my body to bypass the blocked arteries. This technique effectively reroutes blood flow, ensuring that my heart received the oxygen and nutrients it needed to function properly.

The evolution of bypass techniques over the years has significantly improved patient outcomes. Advances in surgical instruments, anesthesia, and post-operative care have made these procedures safer and more effective. Minimally invasive bypass techniques have also emerged, reducing recovery times and minimizing the physical trauma associated with traditional open-heart surgery.

Advancements in Imaging Technologies

One of the critical factors that contributed to the success of my treatment was the advancement in imaging technologies. Modern imaging techniques such as Magnetic Resonance Imaging (MRI) and Computed Tomography (CT) scans have revolutionized the way heart disease is diagnosed and treated.

MRI and CT Scans: These non-invasive imaging technologies provide detailed, high-resolution images of the heart and its surrounding structures. MRI uses powerful magnets and radio waves to create images, while CT scans utilize X-rays to produce cross-sectional views of the body. These technologies allow for precise visualization of arterial blockages, valve abnormalities, and other cardiac issues, enabling doctors to formulate accurate diagnoses and tailor treatment plans effectively.

In my case, MRI and CT scans were instrumental in mapping out the exact locations and severities of my arterial blockages and valve stenosis. This detailed imaging allowed my surgical team to plan the quadruple bypass and aortic valve replacement with remarkable precision, significantly increasing the likelihood of a successful outcome.

Echocardiography and Stress Testing: Beyond MRI and CT scans, advancements in echocardiography and stress testing have also enhanced cardiac care.

Echocardiography uses ultrasound waves to create real-time images of the heart's structure and function, while stress testing evaluates how the heart performs under physical exertion. These tools provide invaluable insights into the heart's health, guiding both diagnostic and therapeutic decisions.

The Evolution of Medical Science

Comparing my father's angioplasty to my own treatment underscores the remarkable progress in medical science. In the early '90s, angioplasty without stents was fraught with higher risks, as seen in my father's case. The introduction of stents—a small mesh tube inserted into arteries to keep them open—revolutionized angioplasty procedures, significantly reducing the chances of complications like restenosis (re-narrowing of the artery).

Stents and Drug-Eluting Stents: The development of bare-metal stents marked a significant advancement, but the real breakthrough came with drug-eluting stents. These stents are coated with medication that helps prevent the growth of scar tissue, further reducing the risk of restenosis. In my treatment, while I did not require a stent during angioplasty, the overall improvement in stent technology contributed to safer and more effective procedures available when my condition was addressed.

Biodegradable Materials: My aortic valve replacement involved a biodegradable repair, a testament to the cutting-edge materials now available in cardiac surgery. These materials not only support the immediate structural needs of the heart but also degrade harmlessly over time, allowing the body's natural tissues to integrate and heal. This innovation reduces long-term complications and enhances the durability of surgical repairs.

Advanced Surgical Techniques: Modern surgical techniques, including robotic-assisted surgery and minimally invasive approaches, have transformed open-heart surgery. These advancements allow for smaller incisions, reduced blood loss, shorter hospital stays, and quicker recovery times. While my surgery required a traditional open-heart approach due to the complexity of my condition, the continuous refinement of these techniques ensures that future procedures will be even safer and more efficient.

Personalized Medicine: The shift towards personalized medicine, where treatments are tailored to an individual's genetic makeup and specific health conditions, has enhanced the effectiveness of cardiac care. Genetic testing and biomarker analysis enable doctors to predict risks, customize treatment plans, and monitor progress with greater accuracy.

Aortic Valve Replacement: Embracing Biodegradable Innovations

Aortic valve stenosis, the narrowing of the aortic valve, posed a significant threat to my heart's functionality. The decision to undergo aortic valve replacement was not taken lightly, but the advancements in valve technology provided a beacon of hope. I opted for a biodegradable aortic repair, a procedure that utilizes materials designed to support the valve while gradually being absorbed by the body.

Benefits of Biodegradable Valves:

- **Reduced Risk of Complications:** Traditional valve replacements can sometimes lead to complications such as infection, blood clots, or rejection by the body's immune system. Biodegradable valves minimize these risks by using materials that the body naturally accepts and processes.
- **Natural Healing:** As the biodegradable material degrades, it allows my body's tissues to grow and integrate seamlessly with the new valve, promoting natural healing and long-term functionality.
- **Longevity and Durability:** These innovative valves are designed to last, providing reliable performance over time without the need for frequent replacements or adjustments.

The success of my aortic valve replacement is a testament to the ingenuity and dedication of modern medical science. It provided not only a solution to my immediate health concerns but also a foundation for a healthier future.

Faith and Medicine: A Harmonious Partnership

Our family's unwavering faith in God has always been a cornerstone of our lives. We believe that God gave us doctors and uses medicine to bring healing to our bodies. Throughout my medical journey, faith was not just a source of comfort but an active participant in the healing process.

Prayer and Preparation: Prayer was an integral part of my preparation for surgery. It provided me with peace of mind and the strength to face the challenges ahead. Whether it was in the quiet moments before surgery or during the lengthy recovery periods, prayer kept me grounded and focused on the positive outcomes we hoped to achieve.

Trusting God and His Word: Trusting in God and His word was fundamental to my preparation. I believed that He had a plan for me and that the medical professionals involved in my care were instruments of His will. This belief reinforced my confidence in the treatment process and helped me navigate the uncertainties that come with major surgery.

Encouragement from Family and Friends: The support and encouragement from family and friends played a crucial role in my recovery. Their prayers, positive affirmations, and unwavering belief in my strength provided the emotional sustenance I needed to endure the physical and mental challenges of surgery and recovery.

Confidence in Medical Professionals: Having complete confidence in my heart surgeon and his team was paramount to my journey. From the initial diagnosis to the post-operative care, their expertise and compassionate approach made a significant difference in my experience.

Transparent Communication: My surgeon did not sugar-coat anything but provided me with honest and detailed information about my condition. This transparency allowed me to make informed decisions about my treatment options. Knowing exactly what to expect helped alleviate fears and enabled me to prepare mentally and emotionally for the surgery.

Expertise and Compassion: The surgical team's expertise was evident in every aspect of my care. Their meticulous attention to detail, combined with genuine compassion, created an environment of trust and safety. They took the time to answer my questions, address my concerns, and ensure that I felt supported throughout the entire process.

Post-Operative Care: The dedication of the medical staff did not end with the surgery. Their commitment to my post-operative care, including physical therapy and regular check-ups, was instrumental in my successful recovery. Their ongoing support exemplified the holistic approach of modern medicine, addressing not just the immediate health issues but also fostering long-term well-being.

The Role of Medical Professionals

The dedication and expertise of the medical professionals who treated my father and me cannot be overstated. Their relentless pursuit of knowledge and commitment to patient care have been instrumental in the advancements that saved my life.

Doctors and Surgeons: The cardiologists and surgeons who managed our cases exemplify the pinnacle of medical expertise. Their ability to diagnose complex conditions accurately and develop effective treatment plans showcases the progress in medical education and training. Their hands-on skills, coupled with their compassionate approach, make a profound difference in patient outcomes.

Nurses and Support Staff: The nurses and support staff provided continuous care, ensuring that both my father and I received the attention and support needed throughout our treatments. Their empathy, patience, and professionalism created a healing environment that extended beyond the technical aspects of medical care.

Researchers and Innovators: The advancements in medical technology and techniques are a direct result of the relentless efforts of researchers and innovators. Their dedication to exploring new frontiers in medicine has paved the way for the life-saving procedures that have become standard practice today. The development of biodegradable materials for valve repairs, for instance, is a testament to their ingenuity and commitment to improving patient care.

Interdisciplinary Collaboration: Modern medicine thrives on interdisciplinary collaboration. The seamless coordination between different specialties—such as cardiology, radiology, surgery, and rehabilitation— ensures comprehensive care for patients. This collaborative approach was evident in my treatment, where a team of specialists worked together to address every aspect of my heart condition.

Impact on Family and Community

Our experiences with heart disease have had profound effects on our family dynamics and our broader community's perception of modern medicine.

Family Dynamics: The diagnosis and treatment of heart disease in both my father and me have strengthened our family bonds. Navigating these health challenges together reinforced our support for one another and deepened our collective resilience. It also heightened our appreciation for life and the importance of health, prompting us to adopt healthier lifestyles and encourage one another to prioritize well-being.

Community Perception: Our family's journey has influenced how our community views modern medicine. Witnessing the stark contrast between my father's treatment and my own has underscored the importance of continued investment in medical research and healthcare infrastructure. It has also highlighted the need for accessible, high-quality medical care for all, regardless of socioeconomic status.

Advocacy and Awareness: Our experiences have inspired us to advocate for better heart health awareness and support for medical advancements. By sharing our story, we aim to educate others about the importance of regular health check-ups, early diagnosis, and the benefits of modern medical treatments. We also emphasize the significance of integrating faith and community support in overcoming health challenges.

Embracing the Future with Hope

As I reflect on these personal narratives, I am reminded of the incredible potential that lies within modern medicine. Each advancement paves the way for new possibilities, offering hope to countless individuals battling similar ailments. The story of my family's encounters with heart disease is a testament to the resilience of the human spirit, the power of faith, and the unwavering progress of medical science.

Looking Ahead: The future of medicine holds even greater promise. Innovations such as gene therapy, artificial intelligence in diagnostics, and regenerative medicine are on the horizon, poised to revolutionize how we understand and treat heart disease. These advancements promise more personalized, effective, and less invasive treatments, further improving patient outcomes and quality of life.

The Importance of Ongoing Research: Continued investment in medical research is crucial for sustaining the momentum of progress. Funding for research initiatives, clinical trials, and technological development ensures that breakthroughs continue to emerge, addressing the evolving needs of patients and combating emerging health threats.

Integrating Faith and Medicine: Our journey has reinforced the harmonious partnership between faith and medicine. As we embrace future medical innovations, we remain steadfast in our belief that both faith and science play integral roles in healing and sustaining life. This synergy provides a balanced approach to health, where spiritual well-being complements physical treatment.

Celebrating the Miracles of Modern Medicine

In celebrating the miracles of modern medicine, we honor not only the scientists and doctors who dedicate their lives to healing but also the faith that sustains us through our darkest hours. Together, faith and medicine continue to work hand in hand, guiding us toward healthier, brighter futures.

Gratitude for Medical Advances: I am profoundly grateful for the medical advancements that saved my life. The ability to undergo a quadruple bypass and receive a biodegradable aortic repair is a direct result of decades of research, innovation, and dedication within the medical community. These procedures have not only extended my life but also enhanced its quality, allowing me to continue cherishing moments with loved ones.

Honoring Medical Professionals: My gratitude extends to the medical professionals who played pivotal roles in my treatment. Their unwavering commitment, expertise, and compassionate care exemplify the best of modern medicine. They embody the spirit of service and the pursuit of excellence that drives the medical field forward.

Faith as a Foundation: Our enduring faith provided the emotional and spiritual foundation necessary to navigate these challenging times. Believing that God had a plan for us and that He worked through medical professionals gave us the strength and courage to face uncertainty with hope and determination.

Inspiring Others: By sharing our story, we hope to inspire others facing similar health challenges to trust in the advancements of modern medicine and to lean on their faith and support systems. Our journey underscores that miracles are not just divine interventions but also the result of human ingenuity and perseverance.

CHAPTER 6
Recovery and Renewal

The Beginning of Recovery

The day after my open-heart surgery marked the start of a challenging yet transformative journey. I had been waiting for my miracle, and God answered my prayers through the skilled hands of my surgical team. Waking up in the hospital, the reality of my situation settled in. The sterile environment, the beeping monitors, and the sight of my loved ones around me were all part of the new reality I had to embrace. The initial moments were filled with a mix of relief and anxiety, knowing that the hardest part was just beginning.

Physical and Emotional Challenges Post-Surgery

Initial Struggles

The first day post-surgery was the toughest. The medical staff encouraged me to sit in a chair, a simple act that felt insurmountable given my weakened state. It was as if I had to relearn how to walk. Every movement was a reminder of my vulnerability, and the effort required for even the smallest tasks was exhausting. There were moments when the difficulty of even the smallest tasks brought me to tears. The frustration of being dependent on others weighed heavily on me, but I knew it was a necessary part of the healing process.

Ongoing Recovery

Every day presented new physical challenges, from regaining strength to managing pain and discomfort. Physical therapy sessions were both grueling and essential, pushing me to my limits while gradually rebuilding my resilience. One day during therapy, I became disheartened because I felt that they were pushing me beyond my capacity, doing the same exercises over and over again from morning until late afternoon. It was really challenging me. I peeled away for a moment to call my wife, and she lifted my spirits, telling me to focus and remember that this is not permanent—it is temporary. I got back there and completed my routine. Emotionally, the journey was a rollercoaster, balancing hope with moments of doubt. There were nights when fear crept in, questioning whether I would ever return to my former self. However, each sunrise brought renewed determination to overcome the obstacles in my path.

The physical toll was immense. Simple movements required deliberate effort, and the pain was a constant companion. There were days when getting out of bed felt impossible, and the mere thought of another therapy session was daunting. Yet, with each passing day, my body began to respond to the treatments. My muscles grew stronger, and my endurance improved. The small improvements were like beacons of hope, illuminating the path ahead.

Leaning on Faith and Family During Tough Moments

Family Support

My wife, Paris McConnell, was my rock, providing unwavering support and encouragement. Her gentle touch and soothing words were a constant source of comfort. Our children—Moses, his wife Alicia, Caleb, and Matthew—along with my grandsons, Jayden and Jordan, were pillars of strength. Their visits filled my hospital room with laughter and love, reminding me of the life waiting for me outside those sterile walls. The first week I was in rehab, a dear friend from Atlanta, Georgia, came and visited me at the facility. He made me laugh, and we had a good time. He also gave me a gift to encourage me, which served as a tangible reminder of the support surrounding me. Extended family members offered their love and assistance, ensuring I never felt alone. Their presence was a testament to the power of familial bonds and unconditional love.

Paris took on the role of my primary caregiver with grace and patience. She managed the logistics of my recovery, from coordinating with medical professionals to ensuring that I had everything I needed. Her unwavering faith in my ability to heal was infectious, inspiring me to push through the most challenging days. The daily interactions with my children and grandchildren brought a sense of normalcy and joy, anchoring me amidst the turbulence of recovery.

Faith as a Foundation

My church family played a crucial role in my recovery. Pastors from Illinois and across the country lifted me up in prayer and spirit. Hebrews 13:5b was a constant reminder: "I will never leave thee nor forsake thee," providing solace during the darkest times. This scripture became a beacon of hope, guiding me through moments of despair and reinforcing my belief that I was never truly alone. During a particularly challenging week, a sermon on hope and perseverance resonated deeply with me, reinforcing my belief that faith could move mountains.

Attending church services, even virtually, kept my faith alive and vibrant, fueling my determination to heal.

Faith became the bedrock upon which I built my resilience. Daily prayers and meditation sessions provided mental clarity and emotional stability. The teachings from the Bible offered comfort and direction, helping me navigate the uncertainties of recovery. Scriptures like Philippians 4:13, "I can do all things through Christ which strengtheneth me," became mantras that I recited during moments of weakness, instilling a sense of purpose and strength.

Community and Compassion

The compassion and sacrifice of those around me made a significant impact. Friends and acquaintances alike reached out, offering meals, prayers, and words of encouragement. I learned through this process that without God, I would not have made it. Without my family, I would not have made it. Without others throughout the Christian community, I would not have made it. Their support alleviated the burdens of daily life, allowing me to focus entirely on my recovery. This outpouring of love highlighted the importance of community and the profound difference it can make in times of need.

One particularly memorable gesture was from a local business owner who organized a fundraiser to help cover medical expenses. The generosity of strangers reaffirmed my belief in the inherent goodness of people and the strength of communal bonds. These acts of kindness, both big and small, created a network of support that was instrumental in my healing process.

Celebrating Small Victories in Your Healing Journey

Milestones Achieved

Each day brought small victories, whether it was sitting up without assistance or taking a few steps. These incremental achievements, though seemingly minor, were monumental in my healing journey. Celebrating these moments kept my spirits high and motivated me to push forward. Every step I took was a testament to my resilience and the unwavering support system surrounding me.

As my strength improved, I began to set achievable goals for myself. From walking a few steps without support to participating more actively in family activities, each milestone was a cause for celebration. These victories were not just physical but also symbolic of my progress and determination. They served as reminders that every effort, no matter how small, contributed to my overall recovery.

Therapeutic Progress

Attending Shirley Ryan Rehabilitation Center was tough but necessary. The rigorous therapy sessions were exactly what I needed to rebuild my strength. Each therapy session felt like a battle, with every movement pushing me closer to reclaiming my strength. The therapists challenged me, encouraging me to surpass my perceived limitations. Celebrating each improvement, no matter how minor, reinforced my commitment to recovery. The center became a place of growth, where determination met compassion, paving the way for a healthier future.

The structured environment of the rehabilitation center provided consistency and discipline, essential components of my recovery. The therapists employed a variety of techniques tailored to my specific needs, ensuring a comprehensive approach to healing. Their expertise and encouragement were invaluable, transforming daunting challenges into manageable tasks. The camaraderie among fellow patients fostered a sense of solidarity, reminding me that I was not alone in my journey.

Transitioning Home: A New Chapter in Recovery

After two weeks of intensive therapy, the day finally came when I made it home. I made it home after two weeks of therapy and continued to improve and get stronger at home. The transition from the rehabilitation center to my own home was both exhilarating and daunting. The familiarity of my surroundings provided comfort, but it also meant that the real work of rebuilding my life was just beginning.

Adjusting to Life at Home

Coming home meant adapting to a new routine. My home had to be modified to accommodate my physical limitations. Ramps were installed to navigate steps, and my living space was reorganized to ensure safety and ease of movement. The first few days were a blend of gratitude and frustration. While I was grateful to be in the comfort of my own home, the realization that my journey was far from over weighed heavily on me.

The adjustments extended beyond physical modifications. Establishing a comfortable and accessible environment was crucial for maintaining the progress I had made in rehab. Simple changes, like rearranging furniture to create clear pathways and setting up a comfortable space for physical therapy exercises, made a significant difference in my daily life.

Continued Physical Therapy

Even at home, physical therapy remained a critical component of my recovery. I worked with a visiting therapist who guided me through exercises designed to strengthen my heart and improve my overall health. The sessions were challenging, often pushing me beyond what I thought I could handle. However, the progress I made was undeniable. Each day, I noticed improvements—greater endurance, increased strength, and enhanced mobility. These advancements were a testament to my perseverance and the unwavering support of those around me.

The home-based therapy sessions provided a sense of normalcy and allowed me to integrate my exercises seamlessly into my daily routine. The personalized attention from my therapist ensured that my workouts were both effective and manageable, preventing burnout and promoting sustainable progress.

Emotional Healing and Mental Resilience

Recovery was not just a physical journey but an emotional and mental one as well. The trauma of surgery and the subsequent challenges tested my mental resilience. There were moments of doubt and fear, but leaning on my faith and family provided the necessary support to navigate these emotional hurdles. My wife, Paris, played an integral role in my emotional healing. Her unwavering belief in my recovery and her constant encouragement were pivotal in maintaining my mental strength.

Therapeutic counseling sessions complemented my physical recovery, offering strategies to cope with anxiety, depression, and the lingering fears associated with my health condition. These sessions provided a safe space to express my emotions and work through the psychological impact of my surgery, fostering a holistic approach to healing.

Strengthening Relationships

Being home allowed me to reconnect with my family on a deeper level. The daily interactions, from sharing meals to engaging in simple conversations, strengthened our bonds. Our home became a sanctuary of love and support, where every member played a role in my healing process. The presence of my children and grandchildren filled our home with joy and laughter, creating an environment conducive to healing and renewal.

These interactions were not merely routine but meaningful exchanges that reinforced our familial ties. Participating in family activities, such as cooking together, playing games, and sharing stories, provided moments of joy and normalcy, essential for emotional well-being. These shared experiences created lasting memories and deepened our connection, serving as pillars of strength during my recovery.

Faith Practices at Home

Maintaining my faith was crucial during this phase of recovery. Daily prayer and meditation became integral parts of my routine, providing solace and guidance. I continued to attend virtual church services, where sermons on hope and resilience resonated deeply with me. These spiritual practices fortified my belief in a higher power and reinforced the message that I was never alone in my journey.

Incorporating faith-based rituals into my daily life,

such as morning prayers and evening reflections, provided structure and a sense of purpose. These practices not only offered spiritual nourishment but also contributed to my emotional stability, helping me navigate the challenges of recovery with grace and strength.

Embracing a New Normal

As weeks turned into months, the concept of a "new normal" began to take shape. I learned to embrace the changes in my life, finding joy in the progress I made each day. The small victories at home—cooking a meal independently, taking a leisurely walk in the garden, or simply enjoying a quiet evening with my family—became milestones in my healing journey. These moments of normalcy were precious, serving as reminders of the life I was rebuilding.

Establishing a Routine

Establishing a daily routine was essential in maintaining my progress. Structured days provided a sense of purpose and direction. Mornings were dedicated to physical therapy exercises, followed by rest and relaxation in the afternoons. Evenings were reserved for family time and spiritual practices. This routine not only facilitated my physical recovery but also contributed to my emotional well-being.

The consistency of a daily schedule helped me stay focused and motivated. By allocating specific times for exercise, rest, and family activities, I created a balanced lifestyle that supported both my physical and mental health. This structure provided a framework within which I could manage my time effectively, ensuring that I remained committed to my recovery goals.

Nutrition and Health

Proper nutrition played a significant role in my recovery. I worked closely with a nutritionist to develop a diet plan that supported heart health and overall wellness. Incorporating wholesome foods, such as fruits, vegetables, lean proteins, and whole grains, became a cornerstone of my daily regimen. Cooking meals became a therapeutic activity, allowing me to take control of my health and contribute to the family's well-being.

The focus on a balanced diet not only aided in my physical recovery but also boosted my energy levels and overall mood. Preparing nutritious meals became an empowering activity, reinforcing my commitment to a healthier lifestyle. Sharing these meals with my family fostered a sense of community and mutual support, enhancing our collective well-being.

Mindfulness and Mental Health

In addition to physical therapy, I incorporated mindfulness practices into my daily routine. Techniques such as deep breathing, meditation, and visualization helped manage stress and anxiety. Mindfulness became a tool for maintaining mental clarity and emotional stability, allowing me to stay focused on my recovery goals.

Engaging in mindfulness exercises provided a sense of calm and centeredness, essential for navigating the emotional complexities of recovery. These practices enabled me to stay present, appreciate the progress I was making, and cultivate a positive outlook despite the ongoing challenges.

Support Beyond the Immediate Family

Extended Family and Friends

Support from extended family and friends continued to play a vital role in my recovery. Regular visits, phone calls, and messages of encouragement kept my spirits high. One particularly memorable visit was from an old friend who brought along a scrapbook of our shared memories, reminding me of the strong bonds and love that surrounded me. These gestures, though simple, had a profound impact on my emotional well-being.

The presence of extended family members provided additional layers of support and companionship. Their involvement in my recovery process ensured that I felt loved and valued, reinforcing the importance of maintaining strong relationships. These interactions served as a constant reminder of the interconnectedness of our lives and the collective effort required for healing.

Community Involvement

Staying connected with my church community provided a sense of belonging and purpose. Volunteering for small tasks at church, such as helping with virtual events or participating in prayer groups, gave me a sense of contribution and fulfillment. Engaging with my community reinforced the idea that recovery was not just a personal journey but a shared one, supported by a network of caring individuals.

Participating in community activities fostered a sense of purpose and engagement, essential for maintaining mental and emotional health. These interactions provided opportunities to give back, express gratitude, and connect with others facing similar challenges. The reciprocal nature of support—both giving and receiving—enhanced my sense of belonging and reinforced the strength of communal bonds.

Professional Support

In addition to family and community support, professional counseling was instrumental in addressing the psychological aspects of my recovery. Therapists provided strategies to cope with fear, anxiety, and depression, helping me build mental resilience. Regular counseling sessions complemented my physical therapy, ensuring a holistic approach to healing.

The insights gained from professional counseling were invaluable in navigating the emotional terrain of recovery. Therapists offered coping mechanisms, cognitive-behavioral techniques, and emotional support that empowered me to manage stress and maintain a positive outlook. This comprehensive support system ensured that all facets of my well-being were addressed, fostering a balanced and sustainable recovery process.

Looking Forward: Hope and Future Plans

Setting New Goals

As my strength and confidence grew, I began setting new goals for myself. These goals ranged from physical achievements, such as completing a full walk without assistance, to personal aspirations, like writing a book about my recovery journey. Setting and achieving these goals provided a sense of accomplishment and direction, motivating me to continue striving for improvement.

The process of goal-setting was empowering, allowing me to take ownership of my recovery journey. Each achieved goal served as a stepping stone toward greater independence and self-confidence. This proactive approach instilled a sense of purpose and direction, essential for maintaining motivation and focus during the later stages of recovery.

Giving Back

Inspired by the support I received, I felt a strong desire to give back to the community. Volunteering became a meaningful way to express gratitude and support others facing similar challenges. Sharing my story through speaking engagements and writing offered hope and encouragement to those in need, reinforcing the importance of community and faith in the recovery process.

Giving back provided a sense of fulfillment and purpose, transforming my personal journey into a source of inspiration for others. Engaging in volunteer work and sharing my experiences allowed me to contribute positively to the lives of others, creating a ripple effect of support and encouragement within the community.

Embracing a Balanced Life

Recovery taught me the value of balance—balancing rest with activity, faith with action, and personal needs with the needs of others. Embracing this balance allowed me to lead a fulfilling life, appreciating the journey of recovery as much as the destination. The lessons learned during this period of healing extended beyond physical health, shaping my outlook on life and relationships.

Achieving balance was pivotal in maintaining long-term well-being. By integrating rest and activity, spiritual practices and daily routines, I cultivated a harmonious lifestyle that supported both my physical and emotional health. This balanced approach enabled me to navigate life's challenges with resilience and grace, fostering a sustainable and fulfilling existence.

Conclusion: Embracing Renewal

Through faith, family, and perseverance, I navigated the arduous path of recovery. Each challenge overcome and each small victory celebrated brought me closer to the miracle I had been waiting for. This journey was not just about healing my body but also about renewing my spirit and strengthening the bonds with those I love. I learned through this process that without God, I would not have made it. Without my family, I would not have made it. Without others throughout the Christian community, I would not have made it. As I look back, I realize that recovery is a testament to the human spirit's capacity to endure, adapt, and flourish even in the face of adversity.

CHAPTER 7

Standing Strong Together: Paris's Story

*W*hen *Mark received his* diagnosis, our lives were instantly impacted. My heart was filled with a mixture of fear, determination, and steadfast faith. This chapter is my story of how we stood strong, anchored in love and faith, as we navigated the path toward healing.

I strive to be a strong woman, but I experienced uncertainty because Mark does not handle challenging news well. I knew I had to be grounded to cope with the adjustments ahead.

Embracing the Role of Support

In the days following Mark's diagnosis, I felt heaviness of responsibility as prepared for a life altering surgery. Proverbs 31:25 (KJV) became a source of strength and inspiration:

> *"Strength and honour are her clothing;*
> *and she shall rejoice in time to come."*

This scripture reminded me that my strength was not just physical but also spiritual and emotional. Embracing my role as support, I focused on fostering an environment of faith and trust within and for our family.

I was encouraged by reading scriptures. I listened to Gospel music. I created playlists of inspirational songs to calm my concerns. Music provides comfort and helped maintain a positive outlook during the most challenging times.

Navigating Emotional Turmoil

Mark's struggles with challenging news, I often bore the brunt of our family's emotional landscape. Proverbs 3:5-6 (KJV) provided immense guidance during these trying times:

> *"Trust in the Lord with all thine heart; and*
> *lean not unto thine own understanding. In*

> *all thy ways acknowledge him, and he*
> *shall direct thy paths."*

I turned to prayer daily, seeking peace and guidance not only for myself but also for Mark and our children. These moments of reflection helped me manage my fears and maintain a sense of calm amidst the chaos.

Strengthening Family Bonds

Amidst the uncertainty, it was crucial to maintain a strong and united family front. Proverbs 31:28-29 (KJV) highlighted the importance of mutual respect and love:

> *"Her children arise up, and call her*
> *blessed; her husband also, and he praiseth*
> *her. Many daughters have done virtuously,*
> *but thou excellest them all."*

I communicated with our *family via texts, emails and conference calls to discuss medical prognosis, feelings, fears, and hopes. Staying connected with our sons fostered an environment of open communication and mutual support, ensuring that our children felt secure, informed and loved despite unknown challenges.*
I organized care for our family. I managed logistics of travel to Chicago for Mark's surgery, hotel stays, and meals for our children and grandchildren. Being

present was essential to sustaining our family and remain supportive.

Building a Prayerful Home

Creating a prayerful home environment was essential in sustaining our faith and hope. Proverbs 15:30 (KJV) underscored the healing power of a cheerful heart:

> *"The light of the eyes rejoiceth the heart:*
> *and a good report maketh the bones fat."*

We incorporated daily prayers and scripture readings into our routine, making faith an integral part of our healing process. This spiritual foundation provided resilience to endure each day with grace and hope.

Leaning on Community Support

Our church community played a vital role in our journey. Proverbs 27:17 (KJV) emphasized the value of mutual encouragement:

> *"Iron sharpeneth iron; so a man*
> *sharpeneth the countenance of his friend."*

Church members offered prayers, meals, and emotional support, creating a network of love and faith that bolstered our spirits. Their unwavering support reminded us that we were not alone in this process and our community stood firm in faith.

Personal Growth Through Adversity

The challenges we faced together fostered significant personal and spiritual growth. Proverbs 16:3 (KJV) encapsulated the essence of our transformation:

> *"Commit thy works unto the Lord, and thy thoughts shall be established."*

Through patience and perseverance, I found a deeper understanding of my own faith and resilience. These experiences strengthened my character and developed more trust in God.

Witnessing Miracles in Everyday Moments

Amidst the trials, there were countless small miracles that reaffirmed our faith. Whether it was a day of improved health, a comforting prayer, or a moment of unexpected joy, these instances served as tangible evidence of God's presence and intervention. Proverbs 18:10 (KJV) became a source of inspiration:

> *"The name of the Lord is a strong tower: the righteous runneth into it, and is safe."*

Each day brought new reasons to believe in miraculous, reinforcing hope and determination to persevere.

A Testament of Love and Faith

This journey is a testament to the enduring power of love and faith. Proverbs 17:17 (KJV) beautifully summarizes the essence of our experience:

> *"A friend loveth at all times, and a brother is born for adversity."*

Love combined with unwavering faith, created an unbreakable bond that carried us through the most challenging times. This bond not only strengthened our relationship but also served as a beacon of hope and inspiration for our family and community.

Moving Forward with Gratitude

As we continue to heal and grow, gratitude remains at the forefront of our hearts. Proverbs 16:8 (KJV) reminds us of the importance of integrity and thankfulness:

> *"Better is a little with righteousness than great revenues without right."*

I am thankful for the support of our family, friends, and church community, recognizing their love and prayers are instrumental in the journey of healing.

Gratitude fuels commitment to live lives that honor God and support others in paths of faith and healing.

Encouragement for Other Women

My encouragement for other women going through similar challenges is twofold:

1. **Find Ten Scriptures That Keep You Centered:**
   o **Practical Steps:**
     ▪ **Write Them Out:** Take time to write each scripture down, allowing the words to sink into your heart and mind.
     ▪ **Print Them Out:** Create printable versions of your favorite scriptures to place around your home, serving as constant reminders of God's promises.
     ▪ **Calendar Alerts:** Add a scripture to your calendar with an alert each day, ensuring that God's word is a daily focus in your life.

2. **Build a Support System with Like-Minded Women:**
   o Surround yourself with women who share your faith and values. Their encouragement

and understanding will be invaluable as you navigate your own journey of faith and healing.

Resources That Helped Me

Scriptures That Strengthened Me:

- **Romans 8:1 (KJV):** *"There is therefore now no condemnation to them which are in Christ Jesus, who walk not after the flesh, but after the Spirit."*

- **John 14:1-3 (KJV):** *"Let not your heart be troubled: ye believe in God, believe also in me. In my Father's house are many mansions: if it were not so, I would have told you. I go to prepare a place for you. And if I go and prepare a place for you, I will come again, and receive you unto myself; that where I am, there ye may be also."*

- **Romans 8:35-38 (KJV):** *"Who shall separate us from the love of Christ? shall tribulation, or distress, or persecution, or famine, or nakedness, or peril, or sword? As it is written, For thy sake we are killed all the day long; we are accounted as sheep for the slaughter. Nay, in all these things we are more than conquerors through him that loved us. For I am persuaded, that neither death, nor life, nor angels, nor principalities, nor powers, nor things present, nor things to come, Nor height, nor depth, nor any other creature, shall be able* to separate us from the love of God, which is in Christ Jesus our Lord."

- **Philippians 1:3-7 (KJV):** *"I thank my God upon every remembrance of you, Always in every prayer of mine for you all making my supplication with joy, For your fellowship in the gospel from the first day until now; Being confident of this very thing, that he which hath begun a good work in you will perform it until the day of Jesus Christ."*

- **Habakkuk 3:16-19 (KJV):** *"I heard, and my heart panted: yea, my lips were moved. A watchman said, I will call upon my beloved; surely I will join myself unto him. God is in his holy temple, and the Lord hath his seat in the heavens. His splendour is like the light: he hath rays of brightness. His expression is like the light of sunrise, and his eyes are like the eyelids of the morning. I will stand upon my watch, and set me upon the towers; I will be looking unto the hills."*

- **Isaiah 59:19-21 (KJV):** *"So shall the righteous man live by his faith: and if he turn away, my soul hath no pleasure in him. And I will be found of them that wait upon me, and I will be glorified among them that seek me. Then shall they cry on me from the world afar, and from the north, and from the west; They shall seek me, and shall not find me; they shall ask me, and I will not answer* them. But I will rejoice in the Lord, I will joy in the God of my salvation."

- **1 Samuel 15:22-25 (KJV):** *"And Samuel said, Hath the Lord as great delight in burnt offerings and sacrifices, as in obeying the voice of the Lord? Behold, to obey is better than sacrifice; and to hearken than the fat of rams. And Samuel said unto Saul, Because thou hast rejected the word of the Lord, he hath also rejected thee from being king over Israel. And Samuel turned again, and went to his house at Ramah: and Saul returned from Mizpah, and came to his house at Gibeah."*

- **1 Corinthians 13:4-8 (KJV):** *"Charity suffereth long, and is kind; charity envieth not; charity vaunteth not itself, is not puffed up, Doth not behave itself unseemly, seeketh not her own, is not easily provoked, thinketh no evil; Rejoiceth not in iniquity, but rejoiceth in the truth; Beareth all things, believeth all things, hopeth all things, endureth all things. Charity never faileth."*

- **Philippians 4:8-9 (KJV):** *"Finally, brethren, whatsoever things are true, whatsoever things are honest, whatsoever things are just, whatsoever things are pure, whatsoever things are lovely, whatsoever things are of good report; if there be any virtue, and if there be any praise, think on these things. Those things, which ye have both* *learned, and received, and heard, and seen in me, do: and the God of peace shall be with you."*

- **Philippians 4:5-7 (KJV):** *"Let your moderation be known unto all men. The Lord is at hand. Be careful for nothing; but in every thing by prayer and supplication with thanksgiving let your requests be made known unto God. And the peace of God, which passeth all understanding, shall keep your hearts and minds through Christ Jesus."*

My Playlist:

"I just want to praise" by Maurette Brown Clark

"Be blessed " by Yolanda Adams

"Blessing, Glory and honor" by Jimmie Thomas

"All that God said" by Dr. Ed Montgomery

"Because you loved me" by Kirk Whalum

"The best is yet to come" by Donald Lawrence

"Bless me (Prayer of Janet)" by Donald Lawrence

"Blessed Assurance"by James Ingram

"Can't thank enough" by Wess Morgan

"In the midst of it all" by Yolanda Adams

"Thank you "by Lisa Page Brooks

"The grateful Chant "by Lisa Page Brooks

"In my name" by Rev. Milton Brunson

"Love has no color" by The winans

"Open my heart" by Yolanda Adams

These songs are a source of comfort and inspiration. Music helped me to Focus on praise and gratitude even during the most difficult times.

Concluding Reflections

Standing strong together, anchored in faith, God navigated the challenging path toward healing. A living testament to the power of trust, prayer, and community support. Looking ahead, I remain steadfast and believe God's miracles are not only possible but are actively unfolding daily.

CHAPTER 8

Encouragement for the Waiting

Introduction

L ife often places us in seasons of waiting—moments where we yearn for a miracle, a breakthrough, or an answer to our prayers. These periods can be challenging, filled with uncertainty and impatience. However, the waiting season is not a void but a vital part of our spiritual journey. It is a time for growth, strengthening our faith, and deepening our relationship with God. This chapter aims to provide encouragement and practical advice for those awaiting their miracles, drawing insights from the preceding chapters and grounding our discussion in scripture and testimonies of answered prayers.

Staying Patient and Faithful in God's Timing

Patience is a Virtue

Patience is often tested during times of waiting, especially when our desires seem delayed or unmet. Yet, patience is more than mere waiting; it is an active trust in God's perfect timing. Scriptures encourage us to remain steadfast:

- **Psalm 27:14 (KJV):** "Wait on the LORD: be of good courage, and he shall strengthen thine heart: wait, I say, on the LORD."
- **Ecclesiastes 3:1 (KJV):** "To every thing there is a season, and a time to every purpose under the heaven."
- **James 5:7-8 (KJV):** "Be patient therefore, brethren, unto the coming of the Lord. Behold, the husbandman waiteth for the precious fruit of the earth, and hath long patience for it, until he receive the early and latter rain."

Trusting in God's Plan

God's timing is impeccable, even when it diverges from our own schedules. Trusting His plan requires faith that He knows what is best for us:

- **Proverbs 3:5-6 (KJV):** "Trust in the LORD with all thine heart; and lean not unto thine own understanding. In all thy ways acknowledge him, and he shall direct thy paths."

- **Isaiah 40:31 (KJV):** "But they that wait upon the LORD shall renew their strength; they shall mount up with wings as eagles; they shall run, and not be weary; and they shall walk, and not faint."

Practical Steps to Cultivate Patience

1. **Prayer and Meditation:** Engage in daily prayer, seeking God's guidance and strength to remain patient.
2. **Scripture Reading:** Immerse yourself in the Word of God to reinforce your faith and understanding of His promises.
3. **Community Support:** Surround yourself with a supportive faith community that encourages and uplifts you.
4. **Gratitude Journaling:** Keep a journal of blessings and answered prayers to remind yourself of God's faithfulness.

Finding Peace in the Waiting Season

Embracing God's Presence

Peace is not merely the absence of anxiety but the presence of God within us. Finding peace during waiting involves recognizing God's sovereignty and His assurance of our well-being:

- **Philippians 4:6-7 (KJV):** "Be careful for nothing; but in every thing by prayer and supplication with thanksgiving let your requests be made known unto God. And the peace of God, which passeth all understanding, shall keep your hearts and minds through Christ Jesus."

- **John 14:27 (KJV):** "Peace I leave with you, my peace I give unto you: not as the world giveth, give I unto you. Let not your heart be troubled, neither let it be afraid."

Developing a Peaceful Mindset

Cultivating peace involves intentional practices that align our minds with God's promises:

1. **Mindfulness and Reflection:** Spend time in quiet reflection, focusing on God's presence and promises.
2. **Worship and Praise:** Engage in worship to shift your focus from your circumstances to God's greatness.
3. **Letting Go of Control:** Surrender your need to control outcomes, trusting that God is handling your situation.

Practical Ways to Experience Peace

- **Daily Devotionals:** Start and end your day with devotionals that center your thoughts on God.

- **Breath Prayers:** Use simple, repetitive prayers like "Lord, have peace" to calm your mind throughout the day.
- **Nature Walks:** Spend time in nature to experience God's creation and find tranquility.

Testimonies of Answered Prayers

Stories of Faith

Nothing inspires hope more than hearing how others have experienced God's intervention. Testimonies serve as powerful reminders of His faithfulness:

- **Abraham and Sarah:** Their long wait for a child, culminating in the birth of Isaac, exemplifies trust in God's timing (**Genesis 21:1-3 (KJV)**).

> "And the LORD visited Sarah as he had said, and the LORD did unto Sarah as he had promised. For Sarah conceived, and bare Abraham a son in his old age, at the set time of which God had spoken to him."

- **Hannah's Prayer:** Hannah's persistent prayer for a child and her ultimate blessing with Samuel highlight the power of unwavering faith (**1 Samuel 1:10-20 (KJV)**).

> "And she was in bitterness of soul,
> and prayed unto the LORD, and
> wept sore."

- **Jesus' Miracles:** The miracles performed by Jesus, such as healing the sick and raising the dead, demonstrate God's ability to intervene in miraculous ways (**Matthew <u>14:13-21</u> (KJV)**).

> "And straightway he charged his
> disciples to have supper with him.
> And they departed thence to the
> other side of the sea."

Modern-Day Miracles

Contemporary testimonies also reinforce the belief in God's ongoing miracles:

1. **Healing from Illness:** Individuals who have overcome severe illnesses through prayer and faith, attributing their recovery to God's intervention.
2. **Financial Breakthroughs:** Stories of people who have experienced unexpected financial provision during times of need.
3. **Relationship Restoration:** Accounts of broken relationships being healed through prayer and divine assistance.

Sharing Your Testimony

Your own experiences can be a beacon of hope for others:

- **Be Honest:** Share both your struggles and how you see God working in your life.
- **Be Specific:** Detail the circumstances and how God's timing made a difference.
- **Be Encouraging:** Aim to uplift others by showing that waiting can lead to miraculous outcomes.

Biblical Examples of Waiting

Joseph's Journey

Joseph's story is a testament to enduring faith amidst prolonged waiting and hardship:

- **Genesis 37-50 (KJV):** Sold into slavery, wrongfully imprisoned, and eventually rising to power in Egypt, Joseph's patience and faith led to his ultimate purpose and the salvation of his family.

  > "But as for you, ye thought evil against me; but God meant it unto good, to bring to pass, as it is this day, to save much people alive."
  > **(Genesis 50:20 (KJV))**

Job's Perseverance

Job's unwavering faith despite immense suffering illustrates the essence of enduring trust in God:

- **Job 1-42 (KJV):** Through loss and grief, Job maintained his integrity and faith, receiving restoration and blessings from God.

  "Though he slay me, yet will I trust in him." (**Job 13:15 (KJV)**)

Daniel in the Lion's Den

Daniel's steadfastness in faith during adversity underscores the rewards of unwavering commitment:

- **Daniel 6 (KJV):** Despite the threat of the lion's den, Daniel's refusal to compromise his faith resulted in divine protection and vindication.

  "My God hath sent his angel, and hath shut the lions' mouths, that they have not hurt me." (**Daniel 6:22 (KJV)**)

Theological Insights on Waiting

Purposeful Delay

God's delays are purposeful, designed to refine our character and align our desires with His will:

- **Romans 8:28 (KJV):** "And we know that all things work together for good to them that love God, to them who are the called according to his purpose."
- **Isaiah 55:8-9 (KJV):** "For my thoughts are not your thoughts, neither are your ways my ways, saith the LORD. For as the heavens are higher than the earth, so are my ways higher than your ways, and my thoughts than your thoughts."

Growth Through Waiting

The waiting period is an opportunity for spiritual growth and preparation:

1. **Character Development:** Challenges during waiting build patience, resilience, and deeper faith.
2. **Dependence on God:** Waiting shifts our reliance from our own strength to God's provision.
3. **Clarity of Purpose:** Time spent waiting can clarify our true desires and God's intentions for our lives.

Eternal Perspective

Viewing our circumstances through an eternal lens helps us understand the transient nature of our trials:

- **2 Corinthians 4:17-18 (KJV):** "For our light affliction, which is but for a moment, worketh for us a far more exceeding and eternal weight of glory; While we look not at the things which are seen, but at the things which are not seen: for the things which are seen are temporal; but the things which are not seen are eternal."
- **Colossians 3:2 (KJV):** "Set your affection on things above, not on things on the earth."

Practical Advice for the Waiting Season

Maintaining Hope

Hope sustains us through uncertainty, keeping our focus on God's promises:

- **Hebrews 11:1 (KJV):** "Now faith is the substance of things hoped for, the evidence of things not seen."
- **Romans 15:13 (KJV):** "Now the God of hope fill you with all joy and peace in believing, that ye may abound in hope, through the power of the Holy Ghost."

Active Waiting

Waiting is not passive; it involves active participation in God's plan:

1. **Seek God's Guidance:** Continually ask for His direction and wisdom.
2. **Stay Engaged:** Remain involved in your community and spiritual practices.
3. **Prepare for Action:** Use the waiting time to develop skills and resources that may be needed when the miracle arrives.

Overcoming Discouragement

Discouragement can derail our faith, but there are strategies to combat it:

- **Remember Past Victories:** Reflect on how God has answered prayers before.
- **Stay Connected:** Engage with supportive friends, mentors, and faith communities.
- **Focus on God's Character:** Remind yourself of God's unchanging nature and His promises.

Developing a Strong Faith

Faith as a Foundation

A strong faith foundation is essential for navigating the waiting season:

- **Hebrews 11:6 (KJV):** "But without faith it is impossible to please him: for he that cometh to God must believe that he is, and that he is a rewarder of them that diligently seek him."
- **Matthew 17:20 (KJV):** "And Jesus said unto them, Because of your unbelief: for verily I say unto you, If ye have faith as a grain of mustard seed, ye shall say unto this mountain, Remove hence to yonder place; and it shall remove; and nothing shall be impossible unto you."

Building Faith Through Practice

Faith grows through intentional actions and experiences:

1. **Consistent Prayer Life:** Regular communication with God strengthens your relationship and trust.
2. **Studying the Bible:** Deepens your understanding of God's nature and His promises.
3. **Obedient Living:** Acting in accordance with God's will reinforces your faith and commitment.

Faith in Action

Putting faith into action demonstrates trust and reliance on God:

- **Stepping Out:** Take bold steps based on God's guidance, even when the outcome is uncertain.
- **Serving Others:** Engaging in acts of service shifts focus from personal desires to God's kingdom.
- **Persevering Through Trials:** Maintain your faith despite setbacks, knowing that perseverance leads to growth.

Encouraging Others in Their Waiting

Be a Source of Support

Your encouragement can uplift others in their waiting seasons:

- **Listen Actively:** Offer a compassionate ear without immediate judgment or unsolicited advice.
- **Share Your Story:** Relate your experiences of waiting and how God has been faithful.
- **Pray for Them:** Lift their needs in prayer, asking God to provide strength and peace.

Dr. Mark and Paris McConnell

Creating a Supportive Community

Fostering a community that embraces and supports waiting seasons benefits everyone:

1. **Small Groups:** Participate in or establish small groups focused on mutual encouragement and prayer.
2. **Mentorship:** Mentor those who are new in their faith or going through tough times, providing guidance and support.
3. **Resources Sharing:** Share books, sermons, and testimonies that inspire and encourage faith.

Practical Ways to Encourage

- **Send Encouraging Notes:** Small gestures of support can mean a lot to someone in need.
- **Invite to Worship:** Include them in community worship and fellowship activities.
- **Celebrate Small Wins:** Acknowledge and celebrate incremental progress and answered prayers.

Embracing Hope for the Future

Hope as a Beacon

Hope shines brightly in the waiting season, guiding us toward the fulfillment of God's promises:

- **Romans 12:12 (KJV):** "Rejoicing in hope; patient in tribulation; continuing instant in prayer;"
- **1 Peter 1:3 (KJV):** "Blessed be the God and Father of our Lord Jesus Christ, which according to his abundant mercy hath begotten us again unto a lively hope by the resurrection of Jesus Christ from the dead,"

Visualizing God's Promises

Visualizing the fulfillment of God's promises can reinforce hope:

- **Imagine the Outcome:** Picture how your life will change once your miracle arrives.
- **Affirm God's Word:** Regularly affirm and declare scriptures that speak to your situation.
- **Stay Positive:** Focus on positive outcomes and God's goodness rather than dwelling on negatives.

Future Glory

Understanding that our present struggles are temporary and leading to eternal glory provides perspective:

- **2 Corinthians 4:16-18 (KJV):** "For which cause we faint not; but though our outward man perish, yet the inward man is renewed day by day. For our light affliction, which is but for a moment, worketh for us a far more exceeding and eternal weight of glory; While we look not at the things which are seen, but at the things which are not seen: for the things which are seen are temporal; but the things which are not seen are eternal."
- **Revelation 21:4 (KJV):** "And God shall wipe away all tears from their eyes; and there shall be no more death, neither sorrow, nor crying, neither shall there be any more pain: for the former things are passed away."

Conclusion

The waiting season, though challenging, is a profound opportunity for spiritual growth, deepened faith, and an intimate relationship with God. By staying patient and faithful, finding peace amidst uncertainty, and holding onto testimonies of answered prayers, we can navigate this period with hope and assurance. Remember, God's timing is perfect, and He is always working behind the scenes for our good and His glory. Embrace the waiting with a heart full of faith, and trust that your miracle is on its way.

Final Encouragement

As you journey through your waiting season, hold onto these truths:

- **God is with you:** Never alone, God walks beside you every step of the way.
- **His promises are true:** Trust in the scriptures and His unfailing word.
- **Miracles happen:** History and testimonies affirm that God still performs miracles today.

May you find strength, peace, and unwavering hope as you wait for your miracle, knowing that God is faithful to fulfill His promises in His perfect time.

CHAPTER 9
A Testimony of God's Grace

In the tapestry of our lives, there are threads of hope, moments of despair, and countless instances where the hand of God weaves His divine plan into our existence. "Waiting for Your Miracle" has been a journey through the valleys and peaks, a testament to patience, faith, and the unmerited favor of God—His grace. This chapter, "A Testimony of God's Grace," encapsulates my personal reflections and experiences, drawing upon the rich material we've explored throughout this book. It seeks to represent not just my story, but also the universal narrative of seeking and receiving God's grace in our lives.

Understanding Grace

Grace, a term often used yet profoundly deep, is the unearned favor of God. It is His gift, not based on our merit, but on His boundless love and mercy. The King James Bible defines grace succinctly:

> *"For by grace are ye saved through faith; and that not of yourselves: it is the gift of God."*
>
> — Ephesians 2:8 (KJV)

This verse underscores the essence of grace— salvation as a gift, not something we can earn. Throughout this book, we have delved into moments where waiting seemed interminable, yet God's grace was at work behind the scenes, orchestrating miracles in His perfect timing.

My Journey of Waiting

My journey was not unlike many others—a path filled with uncertainties, challenges, and the persistent hope for a miracle. Waiting is often misunderstood as passive; however, it is an active pursuit of God's will. In the silence of waiting, I learned to listen, to trust, and to believe in the promises of God.

> *"Wait on the LORD, and be of good courage, and he shall strengthen thine heart: wait, I say, on the LORD."*
> — Psalm 27:14 (KJV)

These words became a mantra during the most trying times. Waiting was not a period of inactivity but a time of preparation, growth, and deepening faith. It was in these moments that God's grace began to manifest in subtle yet profound ways.

Trials and Triumphs

Every trial I faced was a testament to God's sustaining grace. From personal losses to professional setbacks, each challenge was an opportunity to witness God's unwavering support. The Scriptures provided comfort and assurance:

> *"And we know that all things work together for good to them that love God, to them who are the called according to his purpose."*
> — Romans 8:28 (KJV)

This promise became evident as each trial eventually led to growth and new opportunities. God's grace was the steady hand guiding me through adversity, ensuring that every hardship served a greater purpose in His divine plan.

The Power of Prayer

Prayer was the cornerstone of my journey. It was through prayer that I communicated my deepest fears, desires, and gratitude to God. The act of praying was not just a ritual but a profound exchange with the Creator.

> *"Be careful for nothing; but in every thing by prayer and supplication with thanksgiving let your requests be made known unto God."*
> — Philippians 4:6 (KJV)

In moments of doubt, prayer was my refuge. It was through earnest supplication that I experienced the transformative power of God's grace, turning my petitions into realities beyond my imagination.

Miracles in the Waiting

True miracles often defy human understanding, emerging in the most unexpected ways. My story is replete with such divine interventions where waiting transformed into witnessing miracles. These moments reinforced my belief in God's active presence and His ability to turn the impossible into possible.

> *"Jesus looked at them, and saith, With men it is impossible, but not with God: for with God all things are possible."*
> — Mark 10:27 (KJV)

Each miracle, whether big or small, was a clear sign of God's grace. From miraculous healings to unexpected blessings, these events were tangible proof of His enduring faithfulness.

Community and Support

No journey is walked alone. The support of a faith community played a significant role in my experience of God's grace. Fellowship provided encouragement, shared burdens, and collective prayers that amplified the power of divine intervention.

> *"And let us consider one another to provoke unto love and to good works."*
> — Hebrews 10:24 (KJV)

The love and support from others were reflections of God's grace, demonstrating His love through human hands. It was through these relationships that I felt God's presence more keenly, reinforcing the truth that we are never truly alone.

Lessons Learned

Through waiting and experiencing God's grace, several profound lessons emerged:

1. **Patience is a Virtue:** Waiting taught me the importance of patience, not just as a passive act but as an active trust in God's timing.

> *"But they that wait upon the LORD shall renew their strength; they shall mount up with wings as eagles; they shall run, and not be weary; and they shall walk, and not faint."*
> — Isaiah 40:31 (KJV)

2. **Faith Over Fear:** In the face of uncertainty, faith became my anchor, dispelling fears and affirming my reliance on God's promises.

> *"For God hath not given us the spirit of fear; but of power, and of love, and of a sound mind."*
> — 2 Timothy 1:7 (KJV)

3. **Gratitude in All Circumstances:** Embracing gratitude transformed my perspective, allowing me to recognize God's hand in every situation.

> *"In every thing give thanks: for this is the will of God in Christ Jesus concerning you."*
> — 1 Thessalonians 5:18 (KJV)

4. **The Importance of Community:** A supportive community is vital in experiencing and sharing God's grace, providing strength and encouragement during trials.
5. **God's Timing is Perfect:** Understanding that God's timing surpasses our own alleviated the anxiety of waiting, fostering trust in His divine schedule.

Reflecting on Grace

As I reflect on the journey chronicled in "Waiting for Your Miracle," it becomes clear that grace was the underlying theme binding every experience. God's grace was not just a concept but a living, breathing reality that shaped my life.

> *"But he that shall endure unto the end, the same shall be saved."*
> — Matthew 24:13 (KJV)

Endurance, fueled by grace, was the key to unlocking the miracles that awaited. Each step taken in faith was a step towards a deeper relationship with God, a relationship marked by His unending grace.

Sharing the Testimony

This testimony is not merely a recounting of personal experiences but an invitation to others to seek and recognize God's grace in their own lives. It serves as a beacon of hope for those still in the waiting, illustrating that miracles are not just stories but lived realities.

> *"I will declare thy name unto my brethren, in the midst of the congregation will I praise thee."*
>
> — Psalm 22:22 (KJV)

By sharing my story, I aim to inspire others to trust in God's grace, to wait with hope, and to believe in the miracles that He has in store.

Embracing Grace Daily

Living in the light of God's grace means embracing it daily, allowing it to influence our thoughts, actions, and interactions. It calls for a continuous recognition of His presence and an unwavering trust in His promises.

> *"And God is able to make all grace abound toward you; that ye, always having all sufficiency in all things, may abound to every good work."*
>
> — 2 Corinthians 9:8 (KJV)

This abundance of grace empowers us to not only receive but also to extend grace to others, creating a ripple effect of divine love and mercy in the world.

Conclusion

"A Testimony of God's Grace" is the culmination of a journey marked by waiting, faith, and the miraculous interventions of God. It is a reflection of how grace operates in our lives, often unseen but always present, guiding us toward our destiny.

In sharing this chapter, I hope to represent not just my story but the collective experiences of countless individuals who have awaited and received God's grace in various forms. May this testimony encourage you to continue waiting, to trust in His timing, and to embrace the miracles that His grace brings.

> *"Now to him that is able to do exceeding*
> *abundantly above all that we ask or think,*
> *according to the power that worketh in us."*
> — Ephesians 3:20 (KJV)

Let us hold onto this promise, confident that God's grace will lead us to our miracles, fulfilling His divine purpose in our lives.

Conclusion

As I came to grips with the seriousness of my heart condition, I knew that it would take a miracle from God to bring healing to my body. I had to wait for my miracle, trusting God and leaning on His Word. I received my miracle through open-heart surgery, a testament to the power of faith and divine intervention.

I want to encourage you, the reader, to know that whatever miracle you need, trust God. Have faith in Him and believe that your miracle is on the way. Take the necessary steps to fortify your faith and prepare spiritually as you wait on your miracle. Remember the words of Hebrews 11:1 (KJV):

> *"Now faith is the substance of things hoped for, the evidence of things not seen."*

If God can do it for me, He can do it for you.

As I look to the future, I am committed to using my experiences to uplift and support others in their own journeys of faith and healing. May my story serve as a testament to the enduring power of trust, prayer, and community.

I extend my heartfelt thanks to my wife, Paris, our three sons—Moses, Caleb, and Matthew—and my daughter-in-law, Alicia—along with my two grandsons, Jayden and Jordan. My gratitude also goes to all members of New Cornerstone Baptist Church. A special thank you to Sis. Mary Chaney, Bro. James Taylor, and Sis. Lorita Taylor for your unwavering support and prayers. I also want to thank all my family and friends who stood by me, offering prayers, encouragement, and practical assistance. Your love and faith were instrumental in my healing journey.

As I continue to reflect on this journey, I am reminded that God's miracles often come in the most unexpected ways and times. Through faith, community support, and unwavering trust in God's plan, I was able to overcome a daunting health crisis. May my story inspire you to hold on to faith, seek support, and trust in God's miraculous power in your own lives.

About the Author

Dr. Mark A. McConnell was born on February 7, 1963, and raised in Kansas City, Kansas, by devoted Christian parents. From a young age, his faith was central to his life, accepting Christ at the tender age of five. Dr. McConnell's foundational  spiritual upbringing was nurtured at Mt. Zion Baptist Church under the guidance of Dr. C.L. Bachus.

He pursued higher education with a commitment to his calling, earning a Bachelor's degree in Religion and Philosophy from Bishop College in Dallas, Texas, in 1986. He continued his theological education, receiving a Master of Divinity from Midwestern Baptist Theological Seminary in Kansas City, Missouri, in 1989 and completing a Doctor of Theology (Th.D.) in May 2002.

Dr. McConnell has been blessed with a beautiful family. He married Paris McConnell, his steadfast partner and source of strength, on September 2, 1989. Together, they have three sons—Moses, Caleb, and Matthew—and are proud grandparents to Jayden and Jordan McConnell.

Answering the call to preach, Dr. McConnell delivered his first sermon in May 1984 and was ordained in August 1985. His pastoral journey has included leading three congregations: Southside First Baptist Church in Kansas City, Missouri; Prince of Peace Baptist Church in Peoria, Illinois; and currently, New Cornerstone Baptist Church in Peoria, Illinois. His service extends beyond the pulpit, having served two terms as Moderator of the Central Illinois Baptist District Association in Peoria, Illinois. His involvement with the Baptist General State Convention of Illinois spans over 31 years, during which he has held significant positions, including 2nd Vice President of both the Baptist General Congress of Christian Education and the Baptist General State Convention of Illinois.

Dr. McConnell's dedication and unwavering commitment have led to his current role as President of the Baptist General State Convention of Illinois. His passion for this esteemed body is evident in his consistent participation, having never missed a board meeting, annual session, or Congress of Christian Education. He firmly believes that God has positioned him to lead and serve, fostering unity and growth within the convention.

Dr. McConnell's vision is clear: to uphold and advance the legacy of the Baptist General State Convention of Illinois, continuing its history as a leading force among state conventions. Through dedication and collective effort, he is confident that this convention will remain a beacon of leadership, faith, and service.

About the Author

Paris Elaine Riddle-McConnell
native of Kansas City, MO. third
child of six to parents Buddy &
Delores (Chatman) Riddle.

Married Dr. Mark A.
McConnell September 2, 1989.
Proud Mother of three sons
Mark Allen Moses, Caleb Allen Mark, and Matthew
Allen. A Delighted grandmother of Jayden & Jordan

Active member of New Cornerstone Baptist Church.

Youth Director, Married Couples Ministry and
Outreach Coordinator for social media and new
membership.

Active member of Baptist General State
Convention Minister's Wives Fellowship and Woman's
Auxiliary. Central Baptist District Association and
Peoria Area Community Service:

Paris has been a community volunteer since the age of
ten alongside of her parents in Kansas City with Freedom
Inc.-a political action foundation formed to register
and increase Africa- American voter participation.

Additionally, American Red Cross & Thornberry Boys & Girls Club KCMO through College.

She Continues community service in Peoria since 1993 by serving on several Board of Directors: Peoria Public Schools, PTO President at Whittier Primary & Peoria High School, Manual High School, Advisory Board, American Red Cross Advisory Board, Juvenile Justice Council, Safe to Live Commission-Center for Prevention of Abuse, CASA of Peoria County and Peoria Highway Credit Union as Board Chairman for 2 years.

Professional Accomplishments: Retirement Account Investment Manager for Fidelity Security Life Insurance, Equipment Buyer for Burmah Oil-Kansas City Graphics Division, Department & Office Manager Macys Midwest, Illinois Department of Transportation Community Relations/Legislative Liaison to Governor's Office, Project Manager & Media Consultant for RSVP Executive Services, Civic Engagement Manager for Illinois State Treasurer Michael Frerichs and currently, External Affairs manager for Office of Lieutenant Governor Juliana Stratton.

Education: Paseo High School and Penn Valley Community College, Kansas City, MO, University of Kansas, Lawrence, KS- Business Administration/ Accounting

Memberships: Alpha Kappa Alpha Sorority, Inc, Professional Businesswomen-KCMO, WTS-Women in Transportation Society, Illinois Association of Highway

Engineers, NAACP, IMAG-Illinois Minorities in Government, Peoria Downtown Rotary Club, West Bluff Council, Peoria Public School Board member.

Favorite Scripture: *For it is God which works in you to will and do of his good pleasure. Do all things without murmurings and disputing: that you may be blameless and harmless, sons of God without rebuke in the midst of a cooked and perverse nation among whom you shine as lights in the world; Holding forth the word of life; that I may rejoice in day of Christ, that I have not run in vain, neither labored in vain. Philippians 2:13-*

Printed in the United States
by Baker & Taylor Publisher Services